MOMENT

How to Walk Every Day in
the Deepest Love of Christ

Dave Diamond

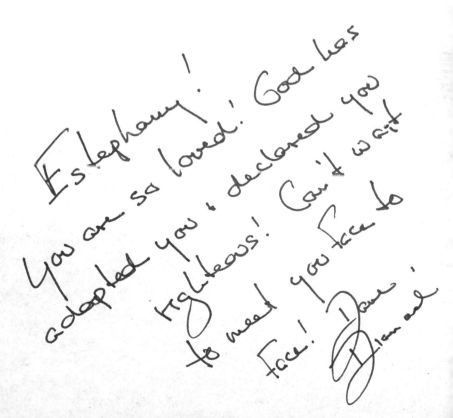

Estephany!
You are so loved!
God has adopted you & declared you
righteous! Can't wait to meet you face to
Face! Dave Diamond

Moment: How to Walk Every Day in the Deepest Love of Christ

David Diamond
P.O. Box 4565
Covington, LA 70434
dave@davediamond.net

Cover Art: I first encountered the presence of Christ at about eight years old in the beautiful church at St. Joseph Abbey in Covington, Louisiana. The interior of that church glows with a stunning series of frescoes painted by Dom Gregory DeWitt, a monk resident at "The Abbey" during the mid 1900's. Elsewhere within The Abbey, I later found a remarkable pastel, also by Dom DeWitt, depicting St. Francis in communion with Christ. The intimate conversation portrayed in that drawing has served as a continuous source of inspiration and comfort to me for a long, long time. I am deeply grateful to Abbot Justin for allowing me to use a detail of Dom Gregory's drawing as the cover artwork for this book.

Dedication

This book is dedicated to my beautiful wife, Debbie, who has put up with my musings about writing a book for four decades. I offer you this dedication, Debbie, in deep appreciation and substantial awe for your continuous grace. You've taught me what love means.

Acknowledgements

I am tremendously grateful for the amazing teachers in my life: Carter Featherston, John Sheasby, David & Vijaya Samuel, Rudy Adkins, William and Lucille of The Elijah Challenge, Beth Baldwin, Thomas Keiffer, Sandip Chauhan, Wanda and Mark Siverd, Barry & Liz Haindel, my sons Sam and Luke, Ayolo David and my "other son" Jeremy Mangerchine.

This is the plain truth: this book would not have been published without the encouragement of Jeremy Mangerchine, Jeff Christian and Ashley Espinal. Jeremy has walked with me, step by step, always believing that I had a worthwhile message to share and has held me accountable to the process. Jeff Christian has been the voice of truth in my life, questioning my suppositions, causing me to think, pushing me to explore with him this marvelous new identity we've inherited. Ashley, whom I taught in sixth grade, has grown up into a woman of grace, beauty and wisdom. Through her own resources, she afforded me the time to complete this process. I deeply value her friendship and respect.

Foreward

By Jeremy Mangerchine,
Author of *The Longest Bridge Across Water*

Some people waltz into your life, have minimal impact, shuffle a few things around, and, before you know it, they're gone, and you don't really mind. Dave Diamond is not one of these people.

Dave is a wrecking ball of genuine love. When your life collides with his, it will likely never be the same. This is because he has a profound gift of being able to cause you to see God and yourself in a completely revolutionary way, and to do so in a very short period of time. You can simply call it "love."

I met Dave a few years back. We had mutual friends. The friends saw that Dave and I shared a mutual passion for knowing the Holy Spirit deeply and partnering with Him to see His love and power manifest in the lives of others. They decided we needed to meet. They were right. A meeting was arranged, and the rest is history. Dave and I have been virtually inseparable ever since. We have traveled the globe together; we have dreamed and processed our ever-progressing lives together. And while we are not attached in any organizational or structural context, our hearts are eternally united in partnership.

Dave is over 30 years my senior, yet he introduces me as his best friend. I know him very well. I can say with confidence and certainty that he walks in integrity that is second to none. I consider it a tremendous honor to be so closely linked with him. And what I immediately recognized when getting to know Dave, that something that kept me wanting to be around him, is what you are about to discover as you read this book. It is Jesus personified.

Dave is a brilliant writer by craft. His monthly newsletter subscribers anxiously await his latest story to show up in their mailbox. We always wonder, "What will the latest chronicled, seemly random Holy Spirit adventure be? What divine direction carried Dave to some podunk Louisiana, one-red-light, barely-recognizable-English-speaking town? And what happened there?"

Knowing this, I wondered what his book would be like. I knew the essence of Dave's heart, but I was curious to see how he would capture and convey that in book form. What he settled on was brilliant.

This book is a daily devotional on Holy Spirit steroids. You likely will not be able to read only one day at a time and will read it over and over and over and over. It is filled with captivating stories, exciting adventure, deep revelation, humor, and vulnerability—all jammed into one power packed book. It is approachable, yet it will knock you on your butt and leave you dazed by the goodness of God, ready for a lifetime of more.

God is all over this book. I literally laughed out loud, cried a little, and rediscovered God in new ways as I read it. I am as proud to attach my name to the content as I am to the author, because, like he and God, they are one in the same.

It turns out this book has the same effect on people's lives that Dave does in person. It will revolutionize your life, if you let it. Dave knows God. His message is to tell you that you can know God too— unhindered and uninhibited. Dive into this book with an open heart, with your mind open to the leading of the Holy Spirit; I promise you that you will end up in places you never thought you would be and you will absolutely love it.

Jeremy Mangerchine

Introduction

How can we know something Scripture says "surpasses knowledge"?

This past week, Chancey Luna, a young man in Oklahoma was handed a life sentence for murdering a college baseball player. From the window of a car in which Luna and three friends said they "were bored," Luna fired a bullet that hurtled almost entirely through the upper torso of 24-year-old Chris Lane. It ripped into his back, fractured two ribs, tore through his esophagus and lungs, blew a hole through his aorta and pulmonary artery, and finally ended its bloody course lodged near his left shoulder. Lane, an Australian national out jogging in the pre-dawn hours near the home of his American girlfriend, was apparently chosen at random by the teens who later argued that they only intended to scare him.

When I started this book, I intended to write a how-to book, helping people to discover their one-ness with the person of Christ and the authority and power which a revelation of our one-ness with Him ignites.

As I finished the rough draft, however, I realized that the book centers more on Christ's love for us. It's really about His inexhaustible passion. It's about that liquid grace which cascades down upon "whosoever will" in such rich torrents that it defies the limits of our ability to receive.

How do we, as humans, come to fully experience God's love? How do we, as Paul prays for the believers at Ephesus, begin to grasp "the breadth and length and height and depth, and to know the love of Christ which surpasses knowledge?" (Eph. 3:18) How do we come to a place where we receive so fully that "His love is perfected in us" (1 John 4:12) and then blossoms forth like wild roses in the lives of people all around us? (Rom. 5:17) How do we walk every day in this exalted position?

We, as American believers, fall hugely short in at least two dimensions.

The first is that, as 21st-century American Christians, we don't know the heart of God. We don't recognize or acknowledge His untamed yearning for profound intimacy with us. We don't receive the inheritance which He endured the cross to win and then lavishes upon us. Like the Jews who were terrified by the thunderous display of God's majesty and authority at Mount Sinai, we most often respectfully decline a meaningful relationship. We trade away reckless passion for ritual and formula, and then hire conscripts to teach us what God presumably says and how we might keep Him at a safe distance but still satisfied.

The bottom line is this: Jesus went to the cross for us. He ransomed us gladly! He gave thanks (1 Cor. 11:24) before He submitted His body to the blood-drenched butchery that was Calvary. He embraced torture and attempted annihilation for the spiritual right to woo us. Christ, now risen, courts us and pours out upon us His promises and gifts. Clearly intent upon drawing us into His palatial bridal chamber, he coaxes us into the very doorway, eager to possess us entirely with His love and affection. Then for whatever reason, we acknowledge His ardor with a peck on the cheek and go on about our business.

We don't know His heart. We don't see or acknowledge or thirst for the "breadth and length and height and depth" of His passion for us.

Secondly, because we don't know His heart, we, as believers, have no way at all to manifest the zealous yearning of His heart to the love-famished world around us. People who don't know love can't share love effectively. We become salt without savor, self-centered saints with haloes of glitter and tin, religious aristocracy who, like Nicodemus, "cannot see the Kingdom of God." (John 3:3)

God, though, still has a message for us to deliver to the culture in which we live. Despite our disengagement, the message remains. That message involves this vital, life-infusing truth: the love of Christ is the very source by which ALL MEN are endued with value.

He, who spoke the far-flung mysteries of our universe into existence and painstakingly paints magical hues within the irises of our own children's eyes, ascribes value to men. He ascribes value. He assigns worth. Our value exists because He delights in us. (Prov. 8:31) He has crowned (adorned) us with honor and glory and set us over the works of IIis hands. (Heb. 2:7) He went to the cross "for the joy that was set before Him." (Heb. 12:2) That joy consists of the legal right for Christ Himself to enter into a recklessly passionate love relationship with you and me. We didn't put him on the cross; He decided that our worth–yours and mine–justified the agony of Calvary, and, in doing so, established once and for all our market value. We are, in fact, worthy because He says we are worthy. He established that at the cross.

Chancey Luna isn't an accident. He's not a freak, an aberration or a misfit. He is the fruit of the culture which bore him. Chancey didn't ascribe value to human life because no one taught Chancey that God Who loves Him delights in Chancey as His creation. Chancey won't learn that at school, believe me. It may very well be that no one else–NO ONE–knows it either within the wide microcosm which birthed and raised up Chancey.

We have not delivered that message.

The truth is that God LOVES us beyond every imagination. Beyond our denominational affiliation or church attendance. Beyond what we hope. Beyond all knowledge. Beyond our most insane expectations. His love is messy and scary and particular yet indiscriminate. He pours out His passion in volumes which make Niagara Falls look like a drippy sink, and He does so upon the most undeserving among us. He loves drunks and prostitutes, He honors convicts and wise guys, He "receives sinners and eats with them!" (Luke 15:2) He gave His blood to secure righteousness for all of us, and He doesn't differentiate between the gravity of a child molester's lust and the petty gossip of old women. He loves those who give into bestial cravings and murder to the same degree that He loves those who simply fear.

He. Loves. All. Of. Us.

His eternal plan, His intent, His goal is to see His love perfected in us. (1 John 4:12) His eternal plan, His intent, His goal is to draw "many sons to glory." (Heb. 2:10)

Including you.

Including me.

Including Chancey Luna.

We need to grasp the love of Christ with such rubber-meets-the-road clarity that it changes not just our worldview but also our behavior and, then, whets the appetites of everyone we encounter. Because Christ in us knows life as valuable, others should discover in us the meaning of grace. In us, they should find hope. We need to pour out, personify, BE the love of Christ for others. We need to live our lives as walking Show & Tells.

I believe that, once we grasp the love which Father God holds for us, we become unstoppable. I believe that when a person who knows the love of Christ opens his or her eyes in the morning, Satan Himself shrieks in frustration. I believe, as God says, that "those who receive of the abundance of grace and the gift of righteousness will REIGN IN LIFE by the one Christ Jesus." (Romans 5:17)

I hope this book wrecks your life. I hope you get so caught up in the swirling typhoon of your Father's love that, when He sets you back down again, you stagger around like a drunk. I hope that, perhaps for the first time, you discover peace. I hope you emerge from Chapter 35 eager to see the power of your Risen Savior manifest through your hands and lips. I hope this book changes the direction of your entire existence.

God bless you!

Chapter 1

"It Is to Your Advantage!"

"But I tell you the truth, it is to your advantage that I go away; for if I do not go away, the Helper will not come to you; but if I go, I will send Him to you." **John 16:7**

A beautiful woman asked me a question 38 years ago.

Looking back, I know this: her one question jolted my life into an entirely new direction. With a cautious smile and piercing Lebanese eyes, that lovely woman kicked open a trap door beneath my feet. My life, careening along in one specified direction for 24 years–PING!–suddenly ricocheted off into unexplored space. I was Alice tumbling down a rabbit hole, Rip Van Winkle opening his eyes, Bilbo slipping on a ring.

Now 38 years later, I wake up almost every morning as one of the most joyful people on the planet. Almost every morning, I open my eyes exhaling prayers of gratitude, shocked by the goodness of God in my life. I walk every day in power I don't understand, joy I don't deserve, rest I never imagined, and peace beyond every expectation. Life has become a breath-taking, exhilarating journey. Today, at age 62, I tell people always, "This is the best season of my life!" But let's go back...

"Are you a Christian?" she asked me. That was it–four words!

"No," I responded. "And who are you to define what 'Christian' means?"

Unfazed, she responded patiently. "Will you give me 60 seconds to rephrase the question?" I nodded slightly, and she went on, "When I ask you 'Are you a Christian?,' what I'm really asking is this: *In your life, is the person of Jesus of Nazareth more alive, more present, more conversational than is your spouse or your best friend? Do you hunger for Him, feel His presence, hear His voice, know His love more on a minute-by-minute basis than you do any other person in your life?"*

"She's nuts," I thought. I chased her off. But she ventured back, and we began a series of discussions which, at first, I enjoyed like an Olympic fencer with a new sparring partner. Weeks later, I prayed with her "to meet Christ." With her, I asked God to introduce Himself to me, to forgive my sins and renew my heart, to let me know Him as my best friend. I became a "Christian," and the initial experience was exhilarating, liberating and peaceful.

Then I got hijacked, more or less, by "religion" for 25 years.

In the past twelve years, I've been liberated all over again. I've rediscovered the power in that woman's question. I've quit "playing church" and discovered my unity with Christ. I've unstrapped myself from an endless roller coaster of religious services, committees, fellowships, small groups, building campaigns, thou-shalt-nots, thou-shalts, and–most importantly–a long roster of religious teachings and expectations.

I truly love church...but I'm not at church "every time the doors open," and I don't feel guilty about it. I've stepped out of evangelism training programs, "impact months" and "evangelism explosions," yet God has let me introduce literally thousands of people on three continents to His Son in the past five years. I've don't limit myself to a tithe and give much, much more than I ever did before. I've discovered new definitions for age-old concepts such as "confession," "peace," "sin," "righteousness" and "grace." I've seen the enemy face-to-face, and I see mind-bending miracles all the time.

And so I go back to the original question: *"In your life, is the person of Jesus of Nazareth more alive, more present, more conversational than is your spouse or your best friend? Do you hunger for Him, feel His presence, hear His voice, know His love more on a minute-by-minute basis than you do any other person in your life?"*

You can, you know. God longs for a love relationship.

Did you know that, more than any other image, God used the image of a bride and groom to illustrate the relationship that He longs to share with you? Did you know "Beulah," an Old Testament name for the Promised Land (Isaiah 62:4) literally means "marriage"? Did you know that when the Apostle Paul proclaims that the Holy Spirit has been given to us as the "earnest' of our inheritance (Eph. 1:14), that Paul's word for earnest is a modern Greek word for an engagement ring? Did you know the Greek word in the Bible for "communion" is also a word for sexual intercourse–that God desires that kind of unity, a no-holds-barred relationship with you, an experience so deep that it's reflected in human terms by the exclusivity and joy of heart-pounding sex?

"Communion?"

Yes. Think about that for a minute.

Jesus came, lived, died and rose again to seduce you, to woo you into a deeply intimate romance. He is an artful lover, intent upon capturing your heart and securing your affections. His dream has ALWAYS been to draw you into a head-over-heels, all-consuming, non-stop love affair.

Think about the apostles. More than anyone else on Earth, they shared a day-to-day relationship with God. They prayed with Him, ate with Him, walked with Him for weeks at a time. They knew His voice. They watched His compassion bubble forth in miraculous healings. They knew his accent, if Jesus snored or talked in His sleep, His favorite food, His pet peeves. John, who called himself "the one whom Jesus loved," (John 13:23) may have regularly reclined at dinner with his head leaning on Jesus' chest, listening to the heartbeat of God incarnate. Imagine that.

Now get this. When Jesus was about to go the cross, He warned the apostles of His imminent departure. As dismay burst forth upon their faces, He shared this shocking truth: it was "TO THEIR ADVANTAGE" that He leave because, if He left, He would send the Holy Spirit to them.

Do you understand the significance of that? Can you grasp that, through the presence of the same Holy Spirit, **Christ will draw you** into a relationship more intimate, more knowing, more "connected" than the twelve apostles <u>ever</u> experienced with Him? Can you comprehend that He offers us MORE than they ever experienced in the three years they shared with Him? Do you understand that this same relationship is not only available to us but is also TO OUR ADVANTAGE in the same way that it was to the apostles?

So what about it? Can you answer that same question? *"In your life, is the person of Jesus of Nazareth more alive, more present, more conversational than is your spouse or your best friend? Do you hunger for Him, feel His presence, hear His voice, know His love more on a minute-by-minute basis than you do any other person in your life?"*

If that kind of relationship with the Lord of the Universe sounds exciting to you, climb aboard. That's our destination.

Give me a few minutes on a regular basis to nudge you toward a life-changing awareness of His passionate love for you. Read and consider the suggested prayer that ends each short chapter, and, if you can make time, consider the simple exercises.

Welcome aboard!

TRUTH:

Since before time began, God has valued your existence and eagerly anticipated your companionship. He changes us profoundly but loves us exactly as you are.

PRAYER & EXERCISE:

If you've never before asked Christ to introduce Himself to you, begin now just by talking with Him. As you talk, lay your life before Him—your dreams and fears, your strengths and shortcomings, your triumphs and your failures. Give yourself to Him and receive cleansing from Him. Let Him wash away anything in you which you or He might perceive as dark or unworthy. Receive His gift of HIS righteousness, a gift which stands as the very doorway into His Presence. Ask Him to breathe His Holy Spirit into your innermost being so that He will live in you, that both you and He will be constantly aware of His indwelling Presence. Then thank Jesus for hearing and answering your prayer. He died to be able to answer this prayer. He will make Himself known to you. Just ask Him.

Can We Really Walk with God?

Chapter 2
If Noah Could, You Can Too.

"Noah walked with God." Gen. 6:9

Years ago, my beautiful wife Debbie and I welcomed a young African student, age 14, to our home in Louisiana from the killing fields of northern Uganda. We hosted Ayolo, a muscular young man as black as pitch and as graceful as a gazelle, in our home through three years of his high school career. It was an amazing, priceless experience.

Ayolo's father had been murdered by Uganda's President Idi Amin, a blood-thirsty psychopath with a taste for human flesh. Ayolo's mother still lived in "the bush" in Uganda, sleeping in a mud hut, cooking over an open fire, and hauling water daily from a creek. Ayolo's primary school was conducted under a breadfruit tree where he learned to write and multiply by drawing in the dirt with a stick. He hunted with a spear, ate ants and peanut-spinach soup, and sometimes hid his younger siblings in the jungle for days at a time to protect them from tribal marauders, the terrifying Karamajong.

As Ayolo burst into our American world, it was like teleporting someone in from another planet. We eased the adjustment by walking and talking together, gently exploring each other's perceptions, each of us offering the other one wisdom out of our own wildly different cultures and experience. He would sometimes slip his hand into mine as we walked, an African sign of trust and affection that I treasured deeply. Sometimes he told me that I talked too much; I usually felt that Ayolo didn't talk enough.

The Scripture says, "Noah walked with God."

Is that possible for you and me? Is it possible for you and I to "walk," moment by moment in the same atmosphere of confidence, peace, wonder and appreciation which Ayolo and I enjoyed in his teenage years? Will God talk with me? Even if He loves me, does He like me? Will He honor me with His friendship?

Yes! Yes! Yes! Yes! Yes! And yes!!!!!

I remember memorizing from a Baltimore Catechism as a second grader that God is holy, omnipotent, omniscient, eternal, good, and to be glorified. But I've come to recognize that, as much as God is all those things, He is also intensely relational. He loves company. He loves companionship. He loves love. He loves me. He loves you!

God created us not just to relate to us but to LOVE us. The reason Jesus endured the agony of the cross was to make possible a heart-to-heart relationship with YOU just as He once enjoyed with Adam in the Garden of Eden–and maybe even more so. He created marriage, in its ideal, to give us a model of that relationship. The most essential biological relationships of life–husband, wife, father, mother, son and daughter–are, for God, simply elaborate Show-and-Tell demonstrations of how He wants to know us.

Think about this.

None of us will ever completely understand the Trinity. Yes, there is only one God, and yet God exists in three distinct persons: Father, Son and Holy Spirit.

Among the many lessons which we can mine out of the Trinity, this one stands out: even if He was alone, God would still be in relationship.

Even by Himself, He exists in three mind-blowing, powerful, loving and listening persons so that His entire existence is like a perfect dance, a divine waltz, each person always complementing, always completing, always moving in perfect peace and unity, always loving, understanding, always affirming the other two partners that make up the entirety of God.

Think about Olympic figure skaters! For all of their endless practice and training, through thousands and thousands of bone-stretching hours of pain and repetition and exhaustion and triumph and tragedy, they achieve what? Three minutes of Olympic perfection? I tell you this: for all of their expertise and wonder, Olympic figure skaters never begin to imagine the seamless beauty, the fluid grace of the Trinity!

And God achieves this grace every second, every minute, for all of eternity with absolutely no practice at all! The interaction of Father, Son and Spirit is flawless, perfect, an entirely unique concert of joyful grace, the ultimate dance of unity and love.

Now get this: He invites us to share in that.

Each of us is called into the smack-dab middle of that dance–into a second-by-second heart-throbbing experience of His peace, goodness, grace, love and passion, even His sense of humor. We are called, invited, requested to be one with Him.

That's what it means to "walk with God."

Thirty years after Ayolo first entered our home, I remember our walks. I remember delighting in his African proverbs. I remember laughing about the eccentricities of Americans, suddenly perceptible to me through Ayolo's eyes. I remember his horrified laughter when I told him, yes, that Americans really did eat frogs...but only the legs. I remember being shocked that he loved country music, and the simplicity of his observation that African tribal music and American country music both were built around the art of story-telling. I remember his casually citing wonderful African proverbs such as, "Mr. Diamond, everyone knows that, when elephants fight, it is the grass which suffers." These things stand out in my mind because of the quality of relationship which we shared in that special time.

That's what God wants with you. Only He wants it all day, every second, for all of eternity.

To fully enter into that reality, to partake in the wonder and magnificence of that interstellar ballet which is the unity of Father, Son and Holy Spirit–that is the prize we're after.

That's the invitation you hold now in your hand.

TRUTH:

Jesus went to the cross to make possible His companionship with you. His invitation to walk with Him, to actually live inside the waltz which plays out every moment between the Father and Son and Holy Spirit, stands before you daily.

PRAYER:

Lord God, thank You that you are a relational God. Thank You that you created me not to use me or judge me or condemn me but to share Your life, Your identity, Your reality, Your passionate love with me. Open my eyes, God, to the reality of Your presence. Let me know You as my daddy, the lover of my soul, my best friend forever. Teach me, Father, how to hear Your voice, know Your Presence and walk in continuous unity with You. This, God, is the desire of my heart.

EXERCISE:

Would you like to become more aware, more cognizant of Christ in the day-to-day circumstances of your life? At night before going to bed or in the morning with your first cup of coffee, consider the upcoming day's events, circumstances in which God might prove Himself real to you. As a form of prayer, scribble just three or four of those on a Post-It note and stick it into your wallet or pocketbook. I write things down like "Hear from my son Sam today" when I find the distance between our house and Sam's college dorm difficult to handle; "Get the Palmer check" for a client who's account is overdue; or "Get into Suzanne's house today" for a Hospice patient who's reluctant to allow me a visit. As the day in question expires, review your list, and see how you can perceive evidence of God's hand and care in the smallest details of your life.

Chapter 3

How to Prepare for This Walk

"I am no longer worthy to be called your son; make me as one of your hired men." **Luke 15:19**

Imagine that, out of the blue, you come into an inheritance–a glorious mansion worth perhaps a hundred million dollars. Every luxury, down to a permanent staff of servants already compensated out of the same inheritance, is yours: furniture, priceless artwork, swimming pool, indoor tennis courts, amazing technology, acres and acres of manicured lawns, fragrant shaded gardens, and a breath-taking view of mountains and ocean out of almost every window in the house.

"Oh my gosh," you think! You gather your meager goods and step through the front door for the very first time. "Sir," the butler graciously speaks, "all that you see here is yours." He waves his arm all around as you stand in the magnificent foyer.

"Whoa!" you breathe back, and you assume by his gesture that he is referring to the entirety of the expansive foyer. Unloading your luggage from the seat of your new Rolls Royce, you move all of your goods into the foyer and set up camp. No pool. No bedroom. No kitchen. No bath. No technology, No tennis courts. No extensive artwork. No gardens. Very limited view. Just the foyer.

As servants come and try to convince you of the true dimension of your inheritance, you insist, "No! No! This is where I belong! This is mine! This is what I was told! This is good! This is enough!" And you live the rest of your ever-loving life without ever seeing or knowing the fullness, the pleasure, the joy of all that has been freely given to you.

Would you wonder at the foolishness of someone who lived in that predicament? Can you imagine someone being so senselessly impoverished?

And yet the planet's chock full, overflowing with good Christians who live exactly this kind of existence.

This is the truth: every treasure of the heavenly realm is ours by in-heritance through Christ. "Fear not, little flock," says Jesus. "It is your Father's good pleasure to give you the Kingdom!" (Luke 12:32) Not some piece of the Kingdom. Not a little shack on the outskirts. Not some tiny undeveloped lot. Not just the foyer! We inherit EVERY-THING! For as long as you live, you'll unwrap gifts, try on clothes, walk in new discoveries. Just open your eyes and believe.

Look back at Jesus' story of the prodigal son, recorded in Luke 15. The younger son, the foolish one ran away to a distant country and blew through his inheritance, pouring out his cash for parties and prostitutes! Finally, he ran out of money and, unable to provide for himself, was sold into bitter servitude! Far from home, he's been deserted by his good-time friends and forced into hard labor under the fist of a heartless pig-farmer. Simply to fend off starvation, he had to battle with hogs over bean husks floating in their rancid slop. Then in an AHA! moment, his need became greater than his shame, and he determined to run away, run home, and cast himself on the mercy of his father–to beg for the status of a slave in his father's house even though he was, in fact, a son! "When he came to his senses, the boy said,...'I will get up and go to my father, and will say to him, 'Father, I have sinned against heaven, and in your sight; I am no longer worthy to be called your son; make me as one of your hired men.'" (Luke 15:17-19)

Yet, upon the young man's return, Jesus tells us, his father, bursting with compassion, hiked up his gown, ran headlong, swept his wayward son into a massive bear hug, kissed him and proclaimed his intent–the father would restore his son to the honor and authority the boy had held before his long nightmare began! The father would return his son–his son! his son! his son!–to all of the privilege of his family name!

But what's next? How does the boy react to his father's grace?

What if the boy had insisted, "No! No, daddy! I am unworthy! I am unworthy! Make me a doorman in your big, glorious house. I'll live in the foyer! Let me camp out in the foyer!" Can you imagine the father's disappointment? Can you see that such an argument not only impoverishes the son but insults, frustrates, even robs the father? Can you see that the root of the young man's insistence would be tragic unbelief–the wrongful, hurtful conviction that somehow his own sin and shame was larger than his father's love and grace?

I tell you this: we all come to the Father as foolish sons, unworthy in our own eyes, dependent upon His forgiveness and grace. But His response is to rush to meet us with reckless abandon, to rip and hurl away our filthy garments and to openly declare us worthy, to bless and empower us, to give us <u>as our inheritance</u> ALL of the riches He possesses.

Listen and believe what the Apostle Paul wrote in his letter to the Ephesians (vs. 1:3): "Blessed be the God and Father of our Lord Jesus Christ who has blessed us (past tense) with EVERY SPIRITUAL BLESSING IN THE HEAVENLY REALM in Christ"!

As we set out to walk with God, we all come like the prodigal–with NOTHING to offer Him except the damaged goods which is ourselves. We are spiritually naked, empty-handed, destitute. Yet everything we need, everything we could possibly use or want, He's packed for us. He holds all of this–the entire Kingdom!–for us as **AN INHERITANCE!**

You're packed. Leave all your baggage behind. You come into this inheritance naked and broke. That's okay. God has packed, crammed, loaded and stockpiled endless storehouses of treasure for you! YOU'RE ALREADY PACKED! "His divine power hath given unto us ALL THINGS that pertain unto life and godliness, through the knowledge of him that hath called us to glory and virtue!" (1 Peter 1:3)

To learn to walk, every moment, with God in this mind-blowing truth–that ALL God possesses is ours by inheritance –is the pivotal center of life. That truth should be where we live, our new home address.

Welcome home!

TRUTH:

God has not received you as a servant but has adopted you as his child. His Kingdom, His inexhaustible riches and authority are now your home address.

PRAYER:

My Abba God, thank You that You love me. Thank You that the quality and dimension of Your love for me exceeds my every expectation, every fear, every reservation. Thank You that, by Your grace, You have made available to me EVERY BLESSING in the spiritual realm, that I no longer have to fear or manage my life on the foundation of my lack and need. Teach me, Father, to live as a son, not a servant, as an heir and not a slave. Teach me to walk, step by step, with You in the gifting that You have provided just for me.

EXERCISE:

What is it that you want? What is the desire of your heart? What is your need? Lay those things before God today and journal (write down) the things you ask of Him. Then be aware of His Presence, His Spirit as He responds to your prayer. He may change your heart so that your desires take a different form or substance. He may simply provide what you ask. Lay your desires before Him and watch carefully for His response.

Chapter 4

We Inherit?

"And if ye be Christ's, then are ye Abraham's seed, and heirs according to the promise." Gal. 3:29

I imagine that by this time, there's a nagging voice whining in the back of your mind, "Dave, what do you mean, 'we inherit'? Inherit? Inherit? I've never inherited anything!"

Ahh! Not so, my brother and sister!

Turn in your Bible to Genesis 15, one of the most glorious chapters in the entire Good Book! We'll start with the first verse! Hold your breath! The key to your inheritance lies here, and it's as rich a legal document as any ever prepared by a thousand Wall Street attorneys!

In the first verse, God appears in a vision to a little pagan man named Abram, later to be re-named "Abraham." In the beginning, there is NOTHING out of the ordinary about this man. He is truly one of us.

"Abram," God says, "I will be your shield and your very great reward." "Your shield" means your protector, your bodyguard, your defense and refuge. And the Hebrew word for "reward" literally means "your paycheck," as in "wealth," "abundance," "complete provision" and "far more than you could ever ask or need."

But Abram is not impressed! There's an intervening issue close to his heart, and it has to do with inheritance. So Abram's response is something like this, "Reward? What is that to me? If You give me all the world's riches, I have no child, no biological heir! Riches are ultimately meaningless! I have no heir except a servant born into my house!"

So God, honoring Abram's need, takes him by the hand and leads Abram outside of his tent into a clear, moonless desert night. "Look up,"

God prompts him, and even this desert nomad is impressed by the brightness of the Milky Way, a billion stars pinwheeling across the desert sky like a chest full of diamonds spilling out onto a blanket of black satin. Abram stands beside the One who breathed it all into existence. "Look up," whispers God, "and count the stars, if you can!"

"Whoa!" thinks Abram! "That would take a thousand years!"

God very clearly whispers back, "So shall your seed be"!

Abram, trying to wrap his mind around this impossible encounter, allows God to see his unbelief. "Lord, how do I know this is true?"

And in answer to that question, God reaches beyond every constraint, every reasonable expectation, stepping far beyond all logic and reason into a realm of pure and blinding grace. He enters into COVENANT with Abram, like a marriage contract, a legal pledge, a formal oath which, from that point forward, God can never break or ignore! That's the rest of this chapter. That's the weird ceremony that has Abram carving up animals, falling into troubled sleep, and watching God like a smoking pot pass between the bloody pieces of meat!

Listen, you may not recognize the word "covenant," but you've been involved with "covenants," and they are critical to understanding life and the Bible. If you've been married, that's a covenant. If you live in a gated subdivision, you signed a covenant. If you picked a scab and mixed your blood with a friend's to become "blood brothers," your unrealized intention was to tie yourselves together in a covenant.

For us, the vital significance of God's covenant with Abram lies in the fact that blood was shed–first in Abraham doing a slice-and-dice on farm animals and then, 1600 years later, in Jesus confirming the same covenant by giving His own blood on the cross!

So why blood?

The blood signifies that whatever covenant gifts and promises are exchanged between the parties involved also extend <u>BY INHERITANCE</u> to children and grandchildren and great grandchildren through endless generations as long as the covenant is remembered. So, when the story is in the Bible, it's going to be remembered for a lo-o-o-o-ong time!

What does that mean? It means that any promise God made to Abraham is still in effect NOW and includes ALL of Abraham's children... right down to you and me!

So are you Abraham's child?

Listen to what the Apostle Paul writes in the third chapter of his letter to the Galatians: ***"If you belong to Christ, then you are Abraham's seed, and heirs according to the promise."*** (Gal. 3:29)

"Promise"? That's THE promise, the covenant, the bloody arrangement sealing the pledge of God to Abram there in Gen. 15. If you've trusted Christ, everything which God promised and did for Abram, He also promised and did for you. You are an heir! You INHERITED the protection, the provision, the righteousness, the position of love and confidence that Abram had...and all you have to do to qualify is believe.

Is that rich or what?

Listen to me when I tell you that the lottery has nothing on this deal, and there's nothing that you buy to win. You just believe! Look! Look! Look! ***"Therefore, the promise comes by faith, so that it may be by grace and may be guaranteed to all Abraham's offspring—not only to those who are of the law but also to those who have the faith of Abraham. He is the father of us all."*** *(*Romans 4:16)

This is the central truth of the Christian faith, that God made promises to all who believe. He sealed those promises, first with the blood of Abram's animals and, eons later, with the blood of His own dear Son. You had nothing to do with it. You don't earn those promises. You inherit them. You can't buy them; you inherit them. Once you have them, you can't be excluded from them because they are yours by inheritance.

All this comes to you simply in exchange for your faith. Your trust.

Your confidence. Your belief.

The entire estate, the whole Kingdom, everything God offers is yours.

Are you there?

Is it real for you?

Do you own this?

This is your inheritance!

TRUTH:

We do not have to earn God's favor or riches. We inherit them.

PRAYER:

Dear Father in Heaven, how in the world can I ever thank You for Your grace and generosity toward me? How can I thank You for the promise made to Abraham and the covenant which extends that same promise to me? How rich am I? How favored am I that I don't have to worry about losing Your blessing, being robbed of Your favor, somehow being excluded from Your grace! I am Your child, a spiritual descendant of Abraham, Your heir simply by faith. I believe, Father, and I trust You! I will be forever grateful for Your towering, overwhelming love for me. Teach me to receive. Teach me to rest in Your love. Teach me to respond in ways that honor our relationship. I am Yours, Father. I am your child.

EXERCISE:

The essence of religion is that we must constantly perform in order to stand in God's favor. That teaching is a lie, a destructive falsehood that actually separates us from God's love for us. We, as believers, stand in God's favor continually because of the inheritance we hold as children of Abraham, children of faith, heirs to the promises of God's favor.

So ask yourself this question: what is it that I do for the purpose of securing God's favor or in order to "keep Him happy"? What am I doing to EARN His favor instead of resting in the fact that, by inheritance, His favor is already mine?

Make a list of four or five of those things and consciously adjust your motivations in performing them. For example, if you've been getting up early to read your Scripture because you think that earns God's favor, start your time tomorrow thanking Him that you already have His favor long before the alarm clock went off. Let your attitude transform that time from an obligation into a celebration. If you've been tithing because you fear He might curse your selfishness, give away much more than your usual tithe this month with this thought: "God will meet my every need because I am His child. I can give freely, not to appease Him or gain his favor but because, as His child, He affords me this opportunity to participate in His work. He is my shield and my great reward."

Chapter 5

How Noah Did It

"By faith, Noah...became an heir of the righteousness which is according to faith" **Heb. 11:7**

What then is the first gift that we inherit?

There were ten old men, traveling Gospel singers, sitting around my pastor's office, inhaling coffee and small-talking in voices and laughter that testified to a lot of years together.

So in comes my pastor, a little portly and filled with all of his customary energy. He greeted the men, got his own cup of joe, small talked a little, and then asked them a question: "Let me get you gentlemen to help me with my sermon this morning. If you got up to the gates of Heaven and St. Peter asked you why in the world he should open up those pearly gates and let you in, what would you tell him?"

"Don't answer that , Joe," breathed one old man, "You ain't goin' there anyways!" The rest laughed and chuckled and then lapsed into an uneasy silence until one volunteered. "Well," he said, "I been a good man pretty much all my life. I been good to my wife, never ran aroun' on her, loved my kids, never spent time in jail. God knows I been to church! Ole St. Peter ought to smell church on me long before I get there!"

Then they went pretty much around the circle, sharing how each had earned himself a place in glory by the "Cosmic Scale Principle," the idea that each man's good deeds were of sufficient value that, set upon God's heavenly scale, they would outweigh the gravity of his sins.

It was an entertaining conversation, but it brought out all the wrong answers. <u>They were wrong, every one of them.</u>

There's not one person ever born that will enter into the Kingdom of

God on the foundation of his or her good works; the Scripture is very clear. "For by grace you have been saved through faith; and that not of yourselves, it is the gift of God; not as a result of works, so that no one may boast." (Eph. 2:8-9)

The first gift we INHERIT is HIS righteousness, HIS absolute inno-cence, the holiness which belongs to Him, the righteousness which we need in order to see the Kingdom of God! We don't earn a place in Heaven; it comes to us by inheritance!

The truth is there are two kinds of righteousness: inherited righteous-ness and earned righteousness. Inherited righteousness saves. Earned righteousness does not. Earned righteousness is a fruitless mirage.

If you read about Noah in the Old Testament, you might come away thinking Noah was "good enough," that his ability to walk with God was earned by his own good behavior–his "earned righteousness." Genesis says, "Noah was a <u>righteous</u> man, <u>blameless</u> in his time; Noah walked with God." (Gen. 6:9) A study of those two words, "righteous" and "blameless," affords other commendable adjectives: "good," "beyond re-proach," "just" and "fair in all of his dealings." Among men, Noah was exceptionally good. But it was NOT Noah's good deeds which afforded him intimacy with God. Noah did NOT walk with God on the foundation of this earned righteousness!

The second kind of righteousness–that which is not earned but inher-ited–comes clear in Hebrews 11. "**By faith,**" the Scripture says, "**Noah became an heir of the righteousness which is <u>according to faith</u>.**" (Heb. 11:7) "Faith" means Noah believed! Like Abraham, Noah "be-lieved God, and God counted it to him as righteousness." (Gen. 15:6)

It's this simple: God didn't walk with Noah because Noah was well behaved. <u>God walked with Noah because Noah believed and, because Noah trusted Him, God then bestowed righteousness–inherited righteous-ness–upon Noah!</u>

The real trick among believers, however, is not so much what gains us entry into this relationship as much as what allows us to stay there. Most Protestant churches delight in sinners UNTIL they receive God's forgiveness. They loudly proclaim, "Come just as you are, and God will save you!" They sing "Just as I Am" as people move down the aisle to be saved. The pastor shouts, "By faith alone–not by works!"

BUT then...as soon as you step up and place yourself in God's hands, the same pastor who just preached about "by faith alone" will tell you everything you "<u>really need to do</u>" as a Christian to hold on to God's divine favor. To please God, you have to read your Bible, maintain your quiet time, quit smoking and drinking, be a greeter, come to the New Members Class, join a small group, etc., etc., etc.

The common line is that entering into salvation is not about works...but, once you're saved, hike up your pants and roll up your sleeves because it's work, work, work to stay here. That's wrong, wrong, wrong! It's as wrong as the answers from the old Gospel singers.

What God wants for you is REST. What God wants for you is peace. What God wants is relationship. God doesn't change His heart, mind or mood toward you based upon your church attendance, your small group, your volunteer service or what you bring to the church social.

Just walk with Him–how hard is that? Listen to Him whisper to you until His voice becomes the only one you really want to hear. Hold His hand. Let Him heal and restore you. Discover the significance of quiet, and you can literally get drunk on the sweetness of His presence. All those other things will follow.

It's not about trying to justify yourself, stammering about how good you were to your spouse or how you stayed out of jail. God didn't fall in love with who you should be; He fell in love with who you are.

Just believe. And then rest.

That's how Noah was able to walk with God.

That's how you will too.

TRUTH:

God didn't fall in love with who you should be; He fell in love with who you are.

PRAYER:

Father, I recognize now that my constant feelings of unworthiness are based upon my own misunderstanding. The ability to walk with You is not based upon my own righteousness, my own good or bad behavior. I can walk with You because You have, of Your own free will, declared me to be righteous. I possess not my own righteousness (because, without You, I had none to offer). I possess YOUR righteousness, perfect, seamless, without fault or blemish, because You have gifted this to me. Thank You! Thank You! Thank You! Teach me to walk now so that my day-to-day life might reflect the truth of this first gift, YOUR righteousness!

EXERCISE:

Listen carefully to the way that so many believers pray, and then reflect upon the underlying assumptions. How often have you begun your own prayers by asking forgiveness for all of your sins? Can you understand now that forgiveness–absolute and total forgiveness–is the very first gift He gave you? Write out a new prayer, one that reflects this truth: He has declared you to be righteous.

Chapter 6

Heirs of God

"Listen, my beloved brethren: did not God choose the poor of this world to be rich in faith and heirs of the kingdom which He promised to those who love Him?" **James 2:5**

Monday dawned in our Hospice office, and Bart, a male nurse stuffed like a holiday turkey with humor and bluster, rolled into our weekly Hospice staff meeting. "Dave, met Benny yet?"

"No, Bart. I'm scheduled to see Benny today."

"Don't waste your time!" he roared, razzing loudly and shaking his bald head. "Benny's got no more spiritual interest than a toilet seat! Cancer, Dave! He's dying of cancer! He and his buddies are locked up in his house, dark as night, smokin' whatever, telling lies, bad-mouthing women, and suckin' down alcohol! It's a shame, Dave! St. Peter himself couldn't talk Jesus to this guy!"

So I headed out to Benny's. Breathing a quiet prayer, I walked into his house. Whoa! The smoky darkness demanded 10 seconds just to let my eyes adjust, and, when I could see, I found Bart had nailed the scene. Windows were drawn. Every light but the TV was extinguished. Oxygen tubes snaked around the floor beneath beer cans, chip bags, take-out plates and greasy Slim-Jim wrappers. Ashtrays overflowed. Two or three guys in tee-shirts and boxers moved toward the corners at the preacher's arrival. And Benny, gaunt and emaciated with a bald bony skull and shockingly long, spider-like arms, had found a nest to die in, propped up in a mountain of cushions on the sofa.

I left an hour later completely frustrated. A second visit two weeks later ended the same way. Two weeks later, I set my jaw and vowed that, today, a 20-mule team wouldn't drag me out before I shared the Gospel with Benny. I strode in, let my eyes adjust, picked my way through the

34

garbage, and pulled up a chair. I crowded in close enough that my knees bumped Benny's, and I threw a question at him. "How you feelin,' Benny?"

Silently and very, very slowly, Benny leaned forward, his gray face stopping inches from mine. He began to speak but stopped, overcome with emotion. His lips quivered. His eyes filled with tears which then cascaded in silent streams down his cheeks. Long moments passed. Finally, his voice emerged in an awe-struck raspy whisper–"Dave, God lo-o-oves me so-o-o much!"

I was shocked. Stunned. Blown away. Sometime between my second and third visits, the Lord Jesus had introduced Himself to Benny and didn't need my help at all! Benny, with little or no Biblical knowledge and no religious experience to speak of, had received a revelation beyond every human expectation. With Paul the Apostle, Benny was suddenly "able to comprehend...the breadth, and length, and depth, and height, and to know the love of Christ, which passeth all knowledge." (Eph. 3:18-19)

From that day, every visit with Benny became a celebration. "Remember," he would tell me each time, "bring a Scripture!"

One day, I explained to him how Christ not only forgave his sin but how Jesus took of His own righteousness, as if He gave away His own cloak, and had already wrapped Benny up in its folds. "Benny," I said, "when you walk into God's throne room, God will smile. He won't see your past. He'll only see Benny, His child, draped in that glorious cloak, a covering knit out of the righteousness of His Son, Jesus. On that, Benny, on the strength of that glorious covering, you can climb unashamed right up into God's lap. He loves you, Benny. He loves you unconditionally."

"I know, Dave. I know. I feel it. It's like He's told me all of this before," he whispered, weeping unashamedly. "I can't wait! I can't wait!"

How many believers ever grasp this gift–unconditional acceptance, blanket forgiveness, transferred righteousness, His amazing presence, His overwhelming love–which God so easily unveiled in Benny's heart, mind and spirit? And what did Benny do to ever deserve this kind of favor? NOTHING! NOTHING!!! NOTHING except, at some point, Benny recognized his need and simply spread out those shockingly long arms and received.

We don't earn; we inherit righteousness by recognizing both our need and the corresponding gift that God in Christ made available to us. We inherit because He adopts us, counts us as His children, grafts us into the spiritual family which began with Abraham way back in Genesis 15.

Listen again to how God closes up Galatians 3: *For you are all children of God through faith in Christ Jesus. All who have been united with Christ in baptism have put on Christ, like putting on new clothes. There is no longer Jew or Gentile, slave or free, male and female. For you are all one in Christ Jesus. ... You are his heirs, and God's promise to Abraham belongs to you. (Gal. 3:26-29 NLT)*

I ask you today, if you have not yet come into a heart-acceptance of this grace, receive. Let the fullness of God's inheritance for you wash over you as it did in some secret moment over Benny. You are liberated from your own sin and all of its spiritual consequences by INHERITANCE and not by PERFORMANCE. Regardless of your past sin, you are absolutely and ridiculously righteous. You are free. You are loved.

When Benny passed, I had the privilege of doing his memorial service. A big circle of friends showed up, most of them in shorts and muscle shirts, sporting tattoos and rat-tails, bringing coolers full of beer, seafood, and an endless supply of hysterical stories about Benny. Milling around beneath an elevated beach-house, we ate crawfish, drank beer, cried a little, and laughed until our sides ached. I shared with them about Benny's last days, and the whole motley crew bowed their heads and prayed with me.

I think both God and Benny were very, very pleased.

TRUTH:

Because of Christ's gift of righteousness, you have unconditional liberty to climb right now into the lap of your Heavenly Father. You can rest there in absolute freedom and total acceptance.

PRAYER:

My Abba Father, teach me to climb into your lap. Teach me to understand and receive the truth that I am totally forgiven, accepted, even treasured in the throne room of my God. I love you, God. Teach me to rest in your peace and acceptance. Reveal to me, as You did to Benny, the depth of Your unconditional love. I love you.

EXERCISE:

Take time to be quiet and imagine what the throne room of God might be like. Once you have some sort of concept in your mind, imagine yourself entering that room, and watch as God looks up and smiles at you. Imagine Him speaking your name. Imagine Him helping you up into His lap. Imagine putting your head back on His chest, shutting your eyes, and feeling His embrace. Rest there until your heart stills and your breathing calms. Once you've come to a position of rest, turn around on His lap and look back on the problems of this day. I think, from that position of favor, you might find your issues look a little less intimidating.

What Does God Really Want from Us?

Chapter 7

"The Look"

"I am my Beloved's, and His desire is for me." **Song of Solomon 7:10**

Dixie Crawford and Calvin Baham were married in a tiny, ancient, wood plank country church which leaned from its foundations about five degrees to the right, seemingly threatening at any time to collapse on to the red-dirt pine-covered hill where it perched. The gray sky threw down cats and dogs in Biblical dimensions throughout the better part of their wedding, and the over-flow crowd of invitees stood outside of open windows and watched the show from under flocks of umbrellas. Dixie and Calvin had 16 bridesmaids, 16 groomsmen, four flower girls and two ringbearers all arrayed in sartorial splendor in pastel dresses, pastel tuxedoes and (for the men) dark sunglasses. The preacher, who was Dixie's uncle, was a showman with a rich stage voice. He performed the greater part of the ceremony in metered verse–"in poverty and health, in sickness and in wealth, in good times and in bad, in happy times and sad..."

It was the best wedding ever, and, as the wedding photographer, I missed the <u>SECOND MOST IMPORTANT</u> shot. I missed "The Kiss."

I was seated in the front row with an old Hasselblad camera that weighed about four pounds, the kind you held at waist level and looked down into. The trigger trembled, cocked and ready, and the lens and aperture were set. I was on this photo like gravy on rice. But as soon as the preacher said to Calvin, "Son, you may now kiss your bride," the whole screen in my camera went dark. When I looked up, about 15 people crowded like a rowdy horde between me and the couple. People had flown forward like buckshot, holding video cameras, lights, Instamatics, Polaroids, Kodak Brownies, tape recorders, anything they had to try to record the moment! It was a mob scene, and I missed the shot!

But...

If "The Kiss" is the SECOND-MOST IMPORTANT SHOT, what's the first, critical, MOST IMPORTANT image of any wedding ceremony?

I'll tell you.

You need to catch "The Look." The Look may be just a single second in every great wedding. It happens, usually coinciding with the vows, when the bride looks at the groom, and her eyes say EVERYTHING. Her look is worth not a thousand but a million words. Sometimes, if you capture that look at the perfect moment, the film in your camera will almost spontaneously burst into flame. It's beautiful, dazzling, the very essence of love and passion.

What "The Look" says is this: "Everything I have or am, I give to you–my heart, all of my material possessions, all of my money, all of my abilities, my hopes, my memories and dreams, my failures and successes, my wisdom and counsel, my creative abilities, my body, my children, my time, everything, everything, EVERYTHING that I ever have been or am now or ever will be or possess. I give you all of this as a sacred gift, without constraint or limitation, in trust and confidence, simply for this reason: because I love you this much."

Whoa! That's "The Look."

That's what we as believers give to Christ.

But now, think about this.

That's what He also gives to us.

That's what He gave us at the cross. That's what you received when, by faith, you embraced His forgiveness, His life, His Holy Spirit. That's why He created you. That's your destiny and your inheritance.

Now, once you just begin to entertain the enormity of His version of The Look, consider this.

The groom in this picture is not just any Johnny-Come-Lately-from-Detroit. This is the Author of Life. This is the One who created Time simply by speaking it into existence. This is God. This is the same God who can whisper and give birth to galaxies. This is the God who can bring down kings and raise up the meek and humble. This is a God who loved you when you threw around His holy name like it was a curse word, who longed for intimacy when you were giving away sexual favors like trinkets, who saw beauty in you when you were in open rebellion, who raised you up out of your own ashes and filth and now offers you, well, EVERYTHING.

Imagine that. Imagine standing, without blemish and without fault because He has restored and sanctified and perfected you. He stands close enough to hold both of your hands. He looks you in the eye, and you hear His voice echo, vibrate and fill up your innermost being. In full knowledge of every aspect of your pathetic history and miserable poverty, He says to you, "Everything I have, I give to you–my heart, all of my possessions, my riches, my abilities, my hopes, my memories and dreams, my victories and successes, my wisdom and counsel, my creative abilities, my body, my children, my time, everything, everything, EVERYTHING that I ever have been or am now or ever will be or possess. I give you all of this as a sacred gift, without constraint or limitation, in trust and confidence, simply for this reason: because I love you this much."

How do you respond to that? What can you do but simply receive?

Think that's over-stated?

Think about this. One day as a young believer, I sat down for about two hours and tried to count the number of books in the Bible where God uses the institution of marriage as a Show-and-Tell to describe His relationship to us. There are 66 books in the Bible, and, in two hours, I found 45 books in which God or Christ is portrayed as the groom and His people as His bride. Three books–Ruth, Song of Solomon and Hosea– are written about almost nothing else. Genesis, the first book, opens with the creation of Adam and Eve as husband and wife, and Revelation, the last book, closes with the Spirit and the Bride saying, "Come, Lord Jesus!" There are hymns about Beulah Land which means "the land of marriage" in Hebrew. And, every time we attend a wedding, we watch as sacred traditions full of images of Christ pass over us, often without our even knowing it.

He–Jesus–is our bridegroom. He is the lover of our souls.

So what does God want from you?

Just to know you.

To enter into relationship with you.

To talk with you.

To listen to you.

To let you experience, to the absolute capacity that our human frames can allow, the fullness of His joy and pride and love in you.

He wants The Look–to watch you open your heart, your mind, your body, your past and present and future to Him in quiet trust, absolute confidence, and heartfelt recognition of His limitless goodness toward you.

Is that a good deal or what?

TRUTH:

God loves you entirely, in complete knowledge of your most intimate secrets and most shameful history, and has given His own life so that He can share His life eternally with you.

PRAYER:

Lord Jesus, I never imagined that You loved me this much. I never pictured You standing before me giving me The Look. I never imagined that You would give so much to ask for my hand, my heart, or invite me to share such deep intimacy with You. I see that question now, Lord. I see that question in Your eyes, and my answer to Your question is 'Yes. Yes. Yes. Everything I have or am, I give to You. EVERYTHING that I ever have been or am now or ever will be or possess, I give to You all of this as a sacred gift, without constraint or limitation, in trust and confidence, simply for this reason: because I love You this much.' Thank You, Lord for Your love. Thank You for Your promises. Thank You for Your life. I am Yours.

EXERCISE:

Take time yourself to look through the Scripture and catalogue as many allusions as you can find to a bride and bridegroom. Place your name and His name into those references. (Keep in mind that, as we are in Christ now, the conditions and judgments of the Old Testament no longer apply to you. He has freed you from all accusation and condemnation.)

Chapter 8

To Know Him

"Let him that glorieth glory in this, that he understandeth and knoweth me." Jer. 9:24

When my son, Sam, was in junior high, he came to me with a puzzled expression. "Dad," he said, "can I ask you a question privately?"

"Sure, son."

"Dad, what does it take to make a woman fall in love with you?"

Whoa! I thought about that for a minute. "It's easy, Sam. All you have to do is listen carefully to her."

"That's all?"

"Yep, Sam. It's guaranteed. Listen carefully to what she says. Care about the things that she cares about. Know what makes her laugh. Know what frightens her. Know what makes her feel good about herself. If you listen carefully and honor her in all of these things, it's guaranteed, bud. She'll fall in love with you."

Go ahead, guys. Ask your wife or girlfriend or even your momma if that was a good answer. She'll look at you like you just asked, "Darlin,' what comes after 'A'?" When she realizes you're serious, she may slap you upside the head, but she'll certainly tell you, "Amen!"

Guys, your bride doesn't go on a honeymoon with you to bounce back and forth between the bedroom and the breakfast bar! Yes, that's great, but that's not the sum total of why she married you! She's not like you! You get off on football and action movies; she likes the Hallmark channel! She gets romantic about sunsets; all you think about is the ducks flying over and how you can't believe you left your gun back in the house. She wants a kiss or flowers because you've been together now for six months, and, when you think about six months, you're think-ing it's time again for an oil change.

Even on your honeymoon, this is true: your eye contact over dinner, holding her chair for her to sit down, your comment on her beauty, your listening to her talk, your focusing entirely on her as you guide her into the restaurant–all of that is as important in many ways as whatever may or may not happen when you get back up to the honeymoon suite.

A successful marriage grows out of a habit of listening, watching, honoring your spouse simply by paying attention to his or her dreams, his or her desires, fears, ambitions, strengths and weaknesses. If you partner with him or her in a moment-by-moment relationship based upon deep appreciation and irrevocable confidence, your life together will flame up into a passionate romance that others will envy and admire.

That's the same thing–the only thing–that God wants from us.

He wants us to know Him. He wants moment-by-moment relation-ship. He wants more than intimacy; He wants unity. He wants to carry you over His threshold and invite you into the very heart of the eternal exquisite dance that simply happens always and everywhere between the Father, Son and Holy Spirit.

Think about the people in the Scripture who knew the very heart of God–King David, the Apostle Paul, Moses. Let's see the importance they placed upon knowing God.

Moses: Moses stands among the three greatest figures of the Old Testament. In perhaps the most astounding story of Moses' life, Moses begs God to show him His glory–that which, God says, no man can look upon and live. But what is Moses' real motivation? What is it that he re-ally wants? Look closely: *"Now therefore, I pray, if I have found grace in Your sight, show me Your way, THAT I MAY KNOW YOU, that I may find grace in Your sight."* (Ex. 33:13)

King David: Characterized by God as "the man after God's own heart," King David broke every stereotype, every expectation, every rule in his headlong pursuit of intimacy with God. At the very end of his life, he called his son and future king of Israel, Solomon, to his side and gave Solomon this deathbed instruction: *"And you, Solomon my son, KNOW THE GOD OF YOUR FATHER (have personal knowledge of Him; be acquainted with and understand Him; appreciate, heed and cherish Him) and serve Him with a blameless heart and a willing mind. for the Lord searches all hearts and minds and understands all the wanderings of thoughts."* (1 Chronicles 28:19 AMP)

Paul the Apostle: In his most intimate letter, Paul writes this about the deepest and most powerful motivation of his life: *"For my determined purpose is that I might know Him (that I may progressively become more deeply and intimately acquainted with Him, perceiving and recognizing and understanding the wonders of His Person more strongly and more clearly), and that I may in that same way come to know the power of His resurrection (which it exerts over believers), and that I may so share His sufferings as to be continually transformed (in spirit into His likeness even) to His death.* (Phil. 3:10 AMP)

Think about this. Throughout the entire creation process, God looked over and over again at the physical realities that He spoke into being–time, light, stars, planets, mountains, seas, oceans, rivers, meadows, kangaroos, wolves, jellyfish, great whales–and, over and over again, He said, "Wow! This is good."

The very first thing He ever described as "NOT good" was this: **"It is NOT good for man to be alone."** (Gen. 2:18) Have you wondered why that is? WHY is it not good for man to be alone?

Let me suggest that perhaps the best answer is this: Because we as men were made in God's image, and God, by His very nature, is intensely relational. God hates isolation. He hates loneliness. He does not want to be alone.

God wants you to know Him. He wants you to delight in His presence, recognize His voice, heed His suggestions, and rejoice in His truth.

He wants to talk to you, not just through the Scripture but in as many other ways as His creative nature can employ. He wants you to reign beside Him, one in mind, one in purpose, one in motivation, one in strength, one in vision, one, one, one, one, one.

God wants to be one with you.

TRUTH:

The greatest worship you can offer to God is simply a passionate desire to know Him.

PRAYER:

Lord Jesus, I want to know You. I want knowing You to be the hallmark, the center, the passion of my life. Teach me to hear Your voice. Teach me to see Your ways. Teach me to walk by faith. Open Your heart to me, God, and I give You permission to open my heart fully and completely, performing whatever surgery my heart needs to grasp Your love and purpose more fully. I love You, God, and I trust You completely. Be the Lover of my soul. Be God in my life.

EXERCISE:

Ask yourself this: what does a person's life look like when he or she really knows God? Do you know such a person? I'm not talking a religious person or rule-minder; I'm talking about a person who reflects in his or her smile and touch and smallest word the very heart of God. As you think about that person, scribble down some of the characteristics of God that you see in his or her life. Ask God then to make you more aware of those qualities as you interact with other people. Ask Him to express those same qualities through you into the lives of others. Then watch what happens.

Chapter 9

Love Letters & Snapshots

"Let the Word of Christ dwell in you richly." **Col. 3:16**

This is a very dangerous chapter.

I'm asking you to read it very carefully and understand very clearly both what I AM saying here and what I AM NOT saying.

I believe in the Bible. The Bible is the Word of God. The Bible is without error, without contradiction, and contains the very essence of God's wisdom for us. Correctly interpreted, it is authoritative. The Bible out-shines in divine revelation, wisdom and truth any other writing to such a degree that even an attempted comparison is absurd. Trying to compare the Bible to ANY other written piece is like compare the raging surface of the sun to a single winking hello from the butt-end of a firefly.

I believe in the Bible. Entirely. Authoritatively. Absolutely.

If that's settled, turn to Paul's letter to the Colossians and read the beginning of verse 3:17. *"Let the Word of Christ dwell in you richly."*

I read that verse to a wonderful Christian physician recently, and then I asked her, "What does Paul mean when he says, 'the Word of Christ'?"

"He means the Scripture," she said

"Wrong," I replied. "That's impossible. He couldn't be referring to the Scripture. When Paul wrote to the Colossians, most of the New Testament hadn't even been written yet. Another 300 years had to go by before what we know as the New Testament was even gathered together and compiled. So, again, what does Paul mean when he says, 'Let the Word of Christ dwell in you richly'?"

I don't think there's any other answer here but this: "the Word of Christ" is the presence of Christ Himself, the Word which became flesh, the indwelling Godhead who has made you a vessel of His infilling.

So what does it mean to let the Presence of Christ Himself "dwell in you richly"?

"Dwell" means live there. Not just stop in. Not camp out. Not fill you up when you take communion, go to church, say a rosary, have your quiet time, or give ten dollars to the panhandler standing on the interstate off-ramp. "Dwell" means to live there continually, to occupy, to inhabit, to make the space your own, to be there when you screw up, when you triumph and when you flop, when you sin and when you are so caught up in His Presence that you get flat drunk on the physical experience.

To dwell where? "In you." In your breast. In your mind. In your heart. In your every conscious moment. In your dreams, your work, your play, your marriage, your friendships, your quiet moments, in times of peace and quiet wonder, and in the stormy turmoil of every-day life. Even in your past, your history, your heritage. In the nano-second which is present, and in your eternal future.

And how is He to dwell there? "Richly." Abundantly. Lavishly. Largely. Extravagantly. With enough presence that He permeates the air around you. With enough grace that people rest simply by standing next to you. With enough immediacy that He rules over every moment, takes every thought captive, and holds you with sufficient intimate familiarity that you respond to His every whisper, move to His slightest embrace, and speak as His voice echoes through your mind.

That's right. "Speak as His voice echoes through your mind." At a bare minimum, you need to know His voice.

I had an experienced missionary tell me once, "Dave, don't tell new believers that they can hear God's voice! It's dangerous! It's irresponsible! You can't do that, Dave!"

Horse-hockey!

Wasn't it Christ who said, "My sheep hear My voice"? (John 10:27)

Look at Christ in John 8:30-32. As Jesus wages a knock-down, drag-out fight with the Pharisees, verse 30 says many of the people who were present "believed on Him." So, in the middle of this battle, almost like He was standing up in a championship boxing match and addressing the ring-side seats between rounds, He speaks to those who have been believed for, what, maybe five minutes? He says to these brand new believers, "If you continue IN MY WORD, you shall be my disciples indeed; and you will know the truth and the truth will set you free."

Even new believers can hear the voice of God.

Remember what I said about the Scripture. Make no mistake: I believe in the authority, inerrancy and divine inspiration of the Bible. But we have to hold the Bible in its proper place.

What does that mean?

Let's say you're a single man, and God leads you into a long distance relationship with a beautiful Godly woman. Both of you love to write, and so you hand-write letters back and forth almost continually, certainly every day and sometimes more than once a day. You pour out your heart in those letters, revealing the innermost depths of your being, giving this young woman access to all of the most secret chambers of your heart–ALL IN WRITING! And she does exactly the same back to you until you are head-over-heels in love with this amazing creation.

After months, she travels to visit you at your home! Wow! How exciting is this? With great joy, you have the chance to introduce her as your fiance to all of your family and friends.

So you walk into your parents' home. Your whole extended family is gathered at the dining room table. Your fiance is standing at your right hand. In your left hand is a box FULL of those precious, glorious, wonderful letters and photographs, love notes and cards which you've exchanged over the course of your long distance relationship!

"Mom, dad, everyone," you say, "this is Gloria!

Then, leaving Gloria silently standing in the shadows, you reach into the box and start pulling out letters and cards and photos and passing those around, gushing and oohing and aahing, reciting particular passages from memory and pointing out details of photos—while, the whole time, Gloria stands, her actual flesh-and-blood presence entirely unacknowledged, quietly watching the whole scene play out!

Hello? Hello?

"Isn't she amazing?" you ask, and you hold up a particularly wonderful snapshot and kiss her image in front of them all...while she still stands silently in the background.

Is this a little weird?

Would you think this scene a little strange?

And yet it happens all the time.

Wonderful, sincere, saved, Bible-centered Christians sit and discuss the Scripture for days, quoting, teaching, illustrating, parsing, translating, poring over God's Word—while, all the time, God Himself watches silently from the background, dying to enter into the conversation, to explain and to empower. Even as they celebrate His life, Christ Himself is excluded by innocent ignorance from His rightful place within their interaction. They simply don't know that God is a relational God, that He speaks to us easily and clearly if we just learn to recognize His voice! They don't know the reality of His Presence!

I am in no way diminishing the importance of the Scripture! Just as Gloria's love letters reveal the intimate secrets of her heart, so the Scripture reveals to us the fullness of God's character and identity. And yet the Scripture is not God Himself. The Scripture was not meant to be a substitute for the living, active, involved presence of the person of Christ in your life. It's important that you learn to draw that line of distinction both to honor God and honor the Scripture!

Will you let the Word of Christ dwell in you richly today?

TRUTH:

God is talking to us almost all of the time. The question is are we hearing and recognizing His voice?

PRAYER:

Lord Jesus, I want to know Your voice. I want to become so familiar and united with You that, when You even whisper the slightest word to me, I want to hear that word with my whole heart and respond in perfect conversation. Teach me, Lord. Open my ears. Open my eyes. Open my heart to Your voice and to Your Word. Teach me, God! I am Yours.

EXERCISE:

Reach out again to one of those people who you feel knows God, whose life exudes the compassion and kindness of Christ. Ask them how they hear God's voice and to share with you some of those listening-to-God experiences.

I also very strongly recommend three books to you by my best friend, a young author of clarity and grace named Jeremy Mangerchine. His first book, about how he first fell into a passionate first-hand relationship with God, is called *The Longest Bridge across Water.* His second book, only about 75 pages, is about how to operate from a position of continual spiritual rest. It's called *The Quitter's Manual.* The third (about to be published at this juncture) is called *The Table and the Chair.* All three are excellent and very inexpensive, especially in an electronic format.

Chapter 10

So What Does God Sound Like?

"My sheep hear my voice." **John 10:27**

All you have to do is look around at the infinite variety of life and landscape on Earth, and you can assume that a God who abounds in such staggering creativity can find a thousand different ways to talk with you.

That's the truth.

In my own limited experience, I've heard an audible voice only once. At pivotal moments in my life, He's also given me very clear visions, ten-second mental videos which suddenly appear in my consciousness like video clips. He's spoken in dreams, through my dad at times, through people with prophetic gifting, through pastors and teachers like Joseph Prince or John Sheasby, through the writings of great hearts like John G. Lake or Norman Grubb, and, very often, through my wife Debbie, our sons, or situations that rise out of our marriage.

Most often, however, He talks to me in two ways: (1) by illuminating passages in the Scripture in perspectives which I never discerned before, and, more often, (2) very directly by employing that "still small voice" to whisper ideas, emotions and words directly into my mind.

As I've come, through practice, to recognize and listen for His voice, I can distinguish His whispers more and more clearly even as I'm engaged in a different conversation or actively involved in some sort of strenuous activity. He likes to talk when we're occupied with routine chores as well; sometimes He gives me complete outlines for sermons when I'm in the shower!

How do I know when God is speaking with me?

I want to suggest an exercise that I gleaned from the most significant Bible teacher in my life.

As we run through our days, a thousand different ideas pop into our minds. Sometimes we'll even pause and think, "Wow! That was spontaneous! Where did that thought come from?" To answer that question, we almost always consider three options: (1) it's God talking; (2) it's the enemy, or (3) it's the ramblings of my own mind and heart.

About 97% of the time, we choose Option C, chuckling to ourselves, "Oh, it's only me!"

But maybe not.

So here's my suggestion in two easy steps:

(1) Erase the Me! "Erasing the me" is the simplest, most practical way to recognize the spiritual dimension of the thoughts and voices in your head. "Erasing the me" means you no longer assume every thought originates with you; when your mind says, "Wow! Where did that come from?" then "Oh, it's just me!" is no longer your default answer.

Almost every spontaneous thought that pops into your mind carries spiritual significance. The vast majority of your thoughts are of one Kingdom or the other, of light or darkness, anchored in Christ or initiated by the enemy. By erasing the me, your eyes will be opened to the spiritual source and significance of much of the mental traffic of your day. You will become, with practice, more and more comfortable and responsive to His voice...and the results are, well, supernatural!

(2) Know How to Discern between God and Satan!

When an idea pops into your mind, it's almost like someone knocking at the door. You immediately want to holler, "Who is it?" If you erase the me, then you're left with two options: God and Satan. So how do you discern which voice is which?

The Devil? After years and years of study, I'm convinced that Satan has only two weapons. All the horror and misery that he causes happen not because he has so many weapons (anger, lust, greed, fear, etc.) but because he's had long eons to practice with the two weapons which are most effective. Those weapons are enumerated in Revelation 12:9-10.

Weapon #1: Deception–Revelation 12:9 says Satan is a liar, which echoes Christ's proclamation in John 8. The enemy lies always, and he's very good at it. Most often, he lies about God. Secondly, he lies about you. He's very subtle as well, so it's always a good idea to pray and ask God for discernment. Even when Satan speaks the truth, he's setting you up for a lie. He is the father of lies.

Weapon #2: Accusation–Revelation 12:10 says Satan is also an accuser. If the voice you're hearing accuses you or anyone else of any wrongdoing, especially if it turns from condemning your actions to condemning your identity, then cast it out as a form of darkness.

"Wait!" you say. "What about when the Holy Spirit convicts me of sin?" We'll talk about this more, but rest assured: in the New Covenant, the Holy Spirit does not accuse, does not "convict" believers. He will caution you and counsel you. He may warn you of potential consequences of some particular course of action. He will not, however, accuse you. He will not shame you. He does not remember your sins and, therefore, can not accuse you of them. (Heb. 8:6-13)

If you're unsure about the source of some particular thought, you can ask yourself these three questions, knowing that a "YES" answer to any one of these questions indicates that the thought which you're entertaining has its roots in the Kingdom of Darkness:

(1) Does it contradict the truth of the Scripture?

(2) Is this thought rooted in any motive other than selfless love?

(3) If I listen to this voice, will the most likely outcome involve hurt to anyone (other than perhaps some embarrassment to myself)?

God? You can know the voice of God, as well, by asking yourself two questions:

(1) Does what I'm hearing line up entirely with the correctly inter-

preted truth of the Scripture?

(2) Is this voice I'm hearing grounded in deep and selfless love?

Here's the Pay-Off! Above all else, God is a lover–deeply relational, profoundly caring, always sensitive to your deepest desires and nagging fears, eager to listen and engage in conversation! He loves to talk! He loves to share! He loves to woo your heart, capture your imagination, and carry you to places of such astounding beauty that you'll wonder sometimes if your mind and heart can endure it.

The Scripture says that, for the JOY set before Him, Jesus endured the cross. (Heb. 12:2)

What was that joy? What could the farthest reaches of space possibly contain that would so capture the heart of God's Son that He would willingly take up His cross and stumble, blood-drained and covered with the saliva of his tormenters, to that craggy knoll of Calvary? For what prize would He stretch Himself out upon the cross, willingly extending His arms to allow brutal men to drive nails through His wrists and feet? For what reward would He endure long hours of horrific agony, gasping and straining for every breath, writhing and pushing upward on the rough-hewn instrument of His death? Why would He do that?

The answer is to know you. To bless you. To share life with you. So that, through you, He could manifest His glorious wisdom to all of the powers of Heaven. So that, with you as His spouse, He can reign and share with you all of the treasures of His Kingdom forever.

If Christ went to the cross to be able to establish a relationship with you, don't you think His voice might be worth hearing? Can you give Him that chance? Can you learn to listen and discern His quiet whisperings?

Can you find time to stop and listen for His voice?

TRUTH:

God is a relational being. He has a voice. He speaks all the time. With a little practice, you'll hear Him.

PRAYER:

Lord Jesus, I want to know Your voice as well as I know my mother's, my spouse's, my child's. Teach me. I invite You, I ask You, I beg You, let me know the fullness of Your love for me and for all mankind. Make me to know Your softest whisper and to respond, in faith, in every circumstance. Let me hear You whisper my name.

EXERCISE:

For one month, erase the me. Journal every day the things that you believe God is telling you, the lessons you learn, the secrets you share.

Chapter 11

The Wedding Night & Procreation

"And Adam knew his wife, and she conceived." **Genesis 4:1**

As much as the world around us is fixated on sex, I don't think we've even begun to understand it.

Why is it so wonderful? Why is sex, shared together within a holy and legitimate relationship, so profoundly rich, so exhilaratingly pleasurable, so deeply exhausting and breath-takingly satisfying? Why is it that we breathe differently talking about it, hyper-ventilate doing it, and breathe with such conscious awareness of peace in the aftermath? How is it that the pleasure goes beyond the physical, the mental, the emotional, even the spiritual to somehow turn the complete spectrum of life into such a glorious typhoon of pleasure? Why is sex so great?

Because God made sex, in its ideal form, to reflect the spiritual interchange, the deep intimacy, the secret exchange, the exhilarating celebration, the giving and receiving, love and abiding appreciation, the blissful unity of soul that should exist not only between husband and wife but also between you and Himself.

Think that's far-fetched?

I don't think so.

Nor did great fathers and teachers of the faith: John Calvin, Jonathan Edwards, Puritan Francis Rouse, John Cotton, Charles Spurgeon, A.W. Tozer, J. Vernon Magee stand as a few among many.

In the Old Testament, God constantly portrayed the unbelief of Israel as a sexual transgression, so that, in His eyes, the worship of other gods was spiritual adultery or prostitution. Read Ezekiel 16, Jeremiah 13 or the entire book of Hosea. Throughout the Old Testament, God longs for intimacy with Israel, calling out through Isaiah, Hosea, Solomon,

Ezekiel, David and Ruth for the kind of passionate single-minded romance shared between lovers. In the Song of Solomon in particular, as the bridegroom praises his lover's lips and breasts, neck and thighs, she cries out, "I am my beloved's, and his desire is for me!" (Song 7:10) As terms of endearment in Isaiah 62, God calls His people "Hephzibah" ("My Delight Is in Thee!") and "Beulah" ("Marriage.")

Over and over again in the New Testament, Jesus is portrayed as the bridegroom and the church as His virgin bride. Jesus chose on purpose to begin His ministry at a wedding, providing an abundance of wine to facilitate the joyful celebration of that union. (John 2:1-11) John the Baptist refers to Jesus as the bridegroom, saying, "He who HAS THE BRIDE–meaning to have and to hold, to possess, to own or to cling to–is the bridegroom." (John 3:29) And the Apostle Paul chides the church at Corinth, "For I am jealous over you with godly jealousy; for I have espoused you to one Husband, that I may present you as a chaste virgin to Christ." (2 Cor. 11:2)

So now let's move from direct reference to allegory.

Consider the ancient Jewish temple, built by King Herod, which dominated the skyline and the day-to-day life of Jews at the time of Christ! A majestic monument to the glory of God and the aspirations of Herod, it was built of sparkling marble with gold ornaments, capable of holding perhaps 100,000 people within its expansive courts, tended daily by hundreds of priests, and stood as the seat of every significant religious ceremony in the most religious culture in the history of our planet.

Deep within this massive structure stood the Holy of Holies, the innermost sanctuary, a 30' x 30' room so sacred that, if a priest ever gained entrance even to the room next door, he did so only once–one time–in his entire life and was NEVER EVER in his whole life permitted to be so close to the actual Holy of Holies again. Whoa!

NO ONE ENTERED THE HOLY OF HOLIES except the High Priest, and he did so only once annually. On the Day of Atonement, with his body washed and spiritually cleansed, he would step behind the massive veil which served as the doorway to the Holy of Holies, walk breathlessly into the room itself, and sprinkle the blood of a lamb there according to God's instruction. By the sprinkling of this blood, judgment for the sins of Israel was pushed back and the people were accepted once again for at least the next twelve months.

When Jesus died on the cross, the Scripture says that same veil in front of the Holy of Holies–a massive, hand-tooled wall of cloth measuring 60 feet high, 30 feet wide and 4 inches thick–was ripped completely in half from top to bottom. Instead of the Jewish High Priest carrying the blood of a lamb into the Holy of Holies, the Scripture says Christ Himself, by His blood, entered into the TRUE Holy of Holies in Heaven and there, with His blood, satisfied the sin-debt owed to God for our sin. The curtain in Jerusalem was torn by the hands of God to symbolize Christ's entrance and the fact that, by His entrance, He had opened the way for all of us who follow Him as children of His Kingdom.

Can you see how the picture of Christ entering the Holy of Holies on our behalf is an allegory very similar to the act of sex itself? Without being too graphic, the bridegroom enters in, and the bride receives Him into her innermost tabernacle, her own Holy of Holies, allowing Him and Him alone to tear the veil and enter fully, received and accepted, for the first time only by blood, to open the way for the birthing of new children! Is it any wonder that, in Ephesians 5:31-32, Paul cries out, *"For this cause shall a man leave his father and mother, and shall be joined unto his wife, and they two shall be one flesh. This is a great mystery: but I speak concerning Christ and the church."*

It is not God's purpose to condemn or accuse you! He endured the cross to wash away every stain of darkness, every blemish of sin from your heart and soul so that NO ONE, least of all Himself, would ever have grounds to accuse you ever again. He bathed you and cloaked you in His own righteousness. Then He woos you, patiently and mindful of your every fear and misconception, to draw you into a heart-pounding, all consuming, entirely captivating, over-the-top passionate, recklessly romantic relationship where His deepest desire is to know you, to love you, to bless you, to care for you, to romance you! He wants to gently and patiently take possession of your heart, your mind, your will, your emotions, your possessions, your past, your present and your future, even your body–and He offers you His Entire Self in return.

Is that good enough?

So what about evangelism?

Let me ask you this question: when you first fell head-over-heels with your spouse, did you set about to make babies by reading each other some tiny comic book about a bridge and how your sins had separated you from God? Did you conceive children according to some denominational handbook, some over-produced video or me-centered presentation, some slick pre-packaged program about how to share your story?

I don't think so.

Ideally, your babies were born or will be born out of the passion that you share as husband and wife, the fruit of your complete and confident submission of your entire self in love and trust to one another. Your children should be the fruit of your unity, conceived in shared joy and brought to maturity in the security and grace of your love for one another.

God's children are the same way.

When you learn to really walk with God, learn to take part fully in that supernatural love affair on the foundation of His declaring you worthy, when you come to experience the joy of that ongoing moment-by-moment conversation, when you can talk with Him with such familiarity and ease that it's as natural as breathing or smiling or walking...

...then others, people who have never heard the name of Christ or who have exhausted themselves on the hamster-wheel of religion, will come to you and tell you, "Share with me whatever it is that you have. Let me in on this secret. Show me the way."

Then you will be an evangelist.

TRUTH:

God loves you with more passion than you ever imagined. Out of that love, you and He will birth others into the Kingdom.

PRAYER:

Lord Jesus, I want to know the depth of Your love for me. To gain that knowledge, I surrender everything to You. Everything. Knock down every wall in my life. Expose and remove any splinters of darkness that I may have embraced, knowingly or unknowingly. Blow away any false religious teachings, all superstitions, every form of fear and doubt, every wrong belief about myself and my Lord. By the power and authority of Your Holy Spirit living inside of me, I curse and renounce and cast away from me, my family and my home any spirit that would stand between You and that knowledge which I seek. Reveal Yourself to me as the lover of my soul. Let me know You, Lord. Let me know You, Lord. Let me know You, Lord.

EXERCISE:

As God reveals the immensity and depth of His love for you, begin to pray that He would show you how to rest in that love, how to come into that place of silent communion that He has reserved only for you. That may take some time and persistence to find and then accustom yourself to easily slipping in and out of that secret spot. But rest in this knowledge: He will guide you there if you sincerely ask Him.

I know many people, women expecially, who have come into a much deeper knowledge of God's love for them through a modern-day retelling of the Biblical story of Hosea. Out of their history, I strongly recommend that you read the book *Redeeming Love* by Francine Rivers.

Chapter 12

Your Passion Statement

"For my determined purpose is that I may know Him." **Phil. 3:10**

Years ago, my best friend and I traveled to Washington D.C. to take part in a huge spiritual gathering. Because we committed at a late date, we had to make reservations in a second-tier hotel in Alexandria, Virginia, nearly 90 minutes from the event. To make matters worse, someone else called and cancelled our reservations...three times.

Finally, the manager of the Alexandria hotel said he had given away our rooms. There was nothing he could do. My friend, an attorney, pressed his case. In the end, the manager called us back to say he had found us rooms in another hotel, rooms for the originally agreed upon $87 per night. Whoa! I gritted my teeth and asked, "Okay. Where are these new reservations?"

"Well, you'll have to stay" he said, apologetically, "in downtown Washington D.C. at the Ritz-Carlton."

The Ritz-Carlton! WHOA! WHAT?!! For a country boy from Louisiana, this was a serious "YAHOOOO!" moment!

Needless to say, the Ritz-Carlton was phenomenal. Every morning when I stepped out of my room into the hallway, a uniformed maid, tending to her cart or a neighboring room, would greet me BY NAME! "Good morning, Mr. Diamond!" Hello?

One day, I stopped and asked her, "Can you tell me if the Ritz-Carlton has a corporate purpose statement?"

"Yes, sir," she replied. She reached into her back pocket, pulled out a small card, handed it to me, and recited from memory the company purpose statement: "The Ritz-Carlton Hotel is a place where the genuine care and comfort of our guests is our highest mission. We pledge to provide the finest personal service and facilities for our guests who will always enjoy a warm, relaxed, yet refined ambience. The Ritz-Carlton experience enlivens the senses, instills well-being, and fulfills even the unexpressed wishes and needs of our guests."

Hello again!

Every great company in America has a corporate purpose statement. The value of a clear purpose statement is that it defines exactly what the people of that corporation hope to achieve on a day-by-day basis. It sets boundaries. It serves to focus energy and planning. By default, it also defines where the company will NOT invest time, resources and energy.

So here's the question: do you have a personal purpose statement?

"Me," you ask? "Personal purpose statement?"

Well, the Apostle Paul had two of them, and I want you to carefully note the vital importance of each!

The first one is found in the Book of Acts, Chapter 26.

Here's the background. Paul was arrested in Jerusalem to save him from men who had vowed to murder him. Paul's jailor, King Agrippa needs to decide what to do with Paul, and he affords Paul an opportunity to speak in his own defense. The apostle is gracious and clever, sharing, in part, how he first met Christ years before on the road to Damascus.

Paul relates how Jesus appeared to him as a stunningly bright light, knocked Paul down and blinded him. There, as Paul lay blinded in the dust literally not knowing what had hit him, Jesus gave Paul a new purpose, a new job description: *"I said, 'Who are You, Lord?' And He said, 'I am Jesus, whom you are persecuting. Rise and stand on your feet; for I have appeared to you FOR THIS PURPOSE, to make you a minister and a witness both of the things which you have seen and of the things which I will yet reveal to you. I will deliver you from the Jewish people, as well as from the Gentiles, to whom I now send you, to open their eyes, in order to turn them from darkness to light, and from the power of*

Satan to God, that they may receive forgiveness of sins and an inheritance among those who are sanctified by faith in Me.'" (Acts 26:15-18)

For the rest of his life, Paul did this. But was that enough? Was God's purpose statement, delivered to Paul on that dusty road, enough? Was God's spoken purpose enough to <u>motivate</u> Paul to persevere through shipwreck, starvation, beatings and stonings, imprisonment and torture?

Consider Paul for a moment. From the moment God called him, NOTHING stopped him. In 2 Corinthians 11, he briefly catalogued hardships Satan had thrown at him to that date–39 lashes five times, bound three times and beaten with a wooden rod, stoned once and left for dead, shipwrecked three times, once floundering about in the sea for "a night and a day." He was imprisoned for years, naked at times, hungry, thirsty, at the mercy of violent weather, opposed by men who vowed to kill him, and forsaken by people he trusted...yet he NEVER stopped sharing the Good News of the One Who had called him.

I don't think Paul's first purpose statement was sufficient to engender this kind of endurance, this kind of indomitable drive. There had to be something else, something entirely unquenchable inside Paul that fed His ruthless, invincible resolve.

The key to that something lies in Paul's second purpose statement. I call it a "Passion Statement" because it's really not about Paul's job description or responsibilities; it's about his motivation. Read this very carefully and slowly. From Gal. 3:10 in the Amplified Bible, this is Paul's Passion Statement:

"FOR MY DETERMINED PURPOSE IS that I may know Him [that I may progressively become more deeply and intimately acquainted with Him, perceiving and recognizing and understanding the wonders of His Person more strongly and more clearly], and that I may in that same way come to know the power outflowing from His resurrection [which it exerts over believers], and that I may so share His sufferings as to be continually transformed [in spirit into His likeness even] to His death."

Whoa! Read that a few more times. Break it down and breathe it in until you taste it.

The Purpose Statement Jesus gave to Paul on the road to Damascus defined what Paul did. He served. He preached. He taught. He evangelized. He discipled. All these things are what Paul did.

The Passion Statement in Philippians 3:10 is not directly about what Paul did. as much as it is about who Paul was. His passion was his inner motivation, the root of his insatiable hunger, the unquenchable thirst that rose up from the very core of his being. This is the commanding ambition which allowed Paul to overcome every obstacle, endure every suffering, and move on past those who accused and abused him.

His hunger to know God turned Paul into an unstoppable force. And, as much horrendous hardship as he endured over years and years, he still says he knew contentment and joy and grace and peace. All of those gifts and a hundred more were but the fruit of a raging, unquenchable fire burning at even a deeper level than his soul or consciousness. Paul had to know God.

What does this magnificent bridegroom of ours desire from us?

To know Him.

To hunger for the revelation of the depths of His heart. To thirst for the experience of His intimate touch. To rest in the ceaseless, faithful flow of His favor toward us. To trust that, in every daunting circumstance or moment of emotional confusion, He is there with us, for us, in us, around us, always in control, always working on our behalf, always reachable and ready to respond to our need.

He wants us to know Him.

He wants us to know Him.

He wants us to know Him.

TRUTH:

The priorities and circumstances of your life will come clear if you embrace your identity and define your passion–that compelling drive which wells up from your innermost being.

PRAYER:

Lord Jesus, thank You for Your love and grace, Your abiding favor toward me. Instill into me and reveal to me my own defining passion, not only a deep love for You but a constant and resounding hunger for Your Presence, for some aspect of You which is uniquely mine. I am Yours, but I want to feel that I am Yours. I know You love me, but I want to feel that You love me. Speak into my heart, Lord. Let the echo of Your words ignite in me a passion that rivals that of Paul, Stephen, Peter, John and all the saints of old.

EXERCISE:

I've adopted Paul's passion statement as my own. In this regard, I make no bones about plagiarism. I too want to know God, and I'm willing to endure whatever that means to go deeper and deeper and deeper into relationship with Him.

But my passion may not be yours. I encourage you to take some time to pray and ask God to give you a customized, personal Passion Statement that will serve as the deepest motivational impetus of your day-to-day life. Write it down. Then keep it where you can refer back to it on a regular basis. Instead of trying to conform your statement to your lifestyle, let God conform your lifestyle to reflect your God-given passion.

Chapter 13

He Gives Gifts

"According as his divine power hath given unto us all things that pertain unto life and godliness." **2 Peter 1:3**

The most often quoted Bible verse in all Scripture, John 3:16, centers on this truth: "For God so loved the world that He gave..." "He gave." "He gave." It is the nature of love to express itself through giving.

So what kind of gifts does God give?

The tragic young singer Janis Joplin made this line famous, "O' Lord, won't you buy me a Mercedes Benz?" I have my own very clear memories of praying as a kid to win the Publishers Clearinghouse Sweepstakes, and how many times have you prayed for your home football or basketball team to win–even as other people in the same park or stadium prayed for the opposing team to triumph? Is this the kind of "gifts" God gives us? I think not...at least primarily.

Make no mistake. God meets our material needs and delights in fulfilling many wants. There is absolutely nothing holy, righteous or admirable about poverty or lack. David began his most popular Psalm with this line: "The Lord is my shepherd; I shall not lack," (Psalm 23:1) and "Jehovah Jireh"–the God who provides–is a legitimate name of God.

At the same time, allowing ourselves to be consumed by concerns or cravings for material goods is not His plan for us either. Jesus encouraged His followers to watch how God clothes the lilies and feeds birds. Then, pointing out how God prizes us so much more highly than lilies or birds, He chided his disciples not to give into fear or greed, self-centeredness or pride about their material well-being. Instead, He says, "Seek first the Kingdom of God and His righteousness, and all these other things will be added unto you." (Matt. 6:33)

As we come to know and love Him, we become more and more aware that Christ does indeed provide for our physical needs and many of our wants. At the same time, the value of those material treasures pales into dust when compared to Kingdom gifts which empower, sustain and encourage us.

Look around. There are many, many, many very affluent people whose daily lives are meaningless and miserable. In the same way, there are millions of people of extremely limited means who know ongoing contentment, joy and personal fulfillment.

Material wealth can bring physical comfort, but, in the long run, the accumulation of such wealth often proves empty and meaningless. It is out of our relationship with Christ that we receive the richest qualities of life. "I am come that they might have life," said Jesus, "and that they may have it more abundantly." (John 10:10)

By most interpretations, the Bible lists 15 "spiritual gifts." They are prophecy, service, teaching, encouraging, giving, administration, mercy, wisdom, knowledge, faith, healing, miracles, speaking in tongues, interpreting tongues, and helps.

But is that God's entire inventory? Is that all He has to offer?

By no means.

For example, I firmly believe one of God's most powerful gifts may be the gift of love, cited in 1 Corinthians 13. The Scripture tells us that, without love, all of His other gifts are worthless! I've met only three or four people who possess the clearly recognizable spiritual gift of love. My son Sam is one of them. When someone fully embraces that particular gifting, other people can feel it in the air all around them.

I remember when Sam was about six years old, we stayed out late fishing. As we drove the old highway home through the dark, our adventure had left us caked with saltwater residue, tired sunscreen, fish slime, dirt and the glow of a great day together. Trying to keep Sam awake, I asked him, "Sam, you are so good at so many things! You read well and love to play video games. You're a monster at board games, excellent at baseball, you play golf with Pawpaw, love to fish, and–wow!–that's just the beginning! If you had to choose just one thing that brings you the greatest happiness and joy–what would that one thing be?"

"That's easy, Dad," he said sleepily. "It's loving you."

Whoa! I almost steered the car into the ditch!

In the intervening 16 years, that sensitivity to issues of the heart has never left him. It's a gift. Like healing, teaching, tongues, etc., etc., etc.

So what other gifts does God provide for us? Joy, peace, patience, kindness, goodness, faithfulness, self-control, courage, hope, protection, wealth, beauty, loyalty, hospitality, intelligence, a proclivity for languages or math or science, worship, praise, music, an ability to write or sing, a love of nature, physical strength, dexterity, health, and on and on and on.

James says, "**Every good thing given and every perfect gift** is from above, coming down from the Father of lights, with whom there is no variation or shifting shadow." (James 1:17) The Apostle Peter writes, "According as His divine power hath given unto us **all things** that pertain unto life and godliness." (2 Peter 1:3) And Paul writes, "Blessed be the God and Father of our Lord Jesus Christ, **who hath blessed us with all spiritual blessings** in heavenly places in Christ!" (Eph. 1:3)

So the first question you might ask God is this, "Lord, exactly what gifts have You given to me?"

Or, if you admire a gifting in someone else and find a persistent desire in your own heart to possess that same gift, then you can ask the Holy Spirit for it.

Paul instructed the church at Corinth that "the gift you should want most is to be able to prophesy." (1 Cor. 14:1 ERV) I saw that gift manifested in astounding ways in my ministry partner, Jeremy Mangerchine, and I made it clear to God that I longed for that gift as well. I was like a kid after cookies. I wanted prophecy. After weeks of prayer, God told me one morning that He had chosen to give me three other gifts instead: healing, long life and "the ability to see men's souls."

"Hey," I thought, "how sweet is this?"

So what gifts do you want?

God gives for at least two reasons.

First, it tickles Him. He loves to give. It's what lovers do, isn't it? "Fear not, little flock," Jesus said, "for it is your Father's good pleasure to give you the Kingdom." (Luke 12:32)

Second, He lavishes His gifts upon you so that, through you, He can pour His love into the lives of others. He blesses you so that, through you, He can demonstrate His desire, His passion, His grace, and generosity to other people. He loves you in order to woo others into deeper relationship, deeper confidence, deeper trust in Him.

Read Acts 2. When the Holy Spirit first came in power to the apostles, He put on a show. There was the sound of a mighty rushing wind. There were tongues of fire. There were men speaking in one language and an audience hearing them in dozens of different tongues. But, of all of the immediate signs and wonders, there was no evidence of the Presence of God stronger than the one recorded in verses 44-45: "And all those who had believed were together and had all things in common; and they began selling their property and possessions and were sharing them with all, as anyone might have need."

It is the nature of love to express itself through giving. It is the nature of deeper love to give more, and to give it freely and lavishly.

Drawing upon the full measure of His own boundless resources, God's intent is to lavish His goodness upon you so, through you, He can make His goodness and glory known to everyone around you.

That, my friend, is one of the deepest truths of the Scripture.

TRUTH:

God loves you completely and delights in blessing you. In turn, you honor Him by sharing from His generous gifting with everyone who surrounds you.

PRAYER:

Lord Jesus, I recognize that the gifts which You have given to me are provided to me for my joy and the joy of all who surround me. I thank You that, by Your gifting, I can reflect the goodness of Your nature, the generosity of Your heart, the unfailing wonder of Your love for even the least of men. Teach me, Father, to walk with confidence as a member of Your royal family. Teach me to serve as an avenue for your largesse. Teach me, Father, to manifest Your heart and nature to all the world around me.

EXERCISE:

Go online and pull up an "inventory of spiritual gifts." Complete that, and see if there's anything there which surprises you. Ask your friends and family members about the gifts and abilities which God has given them and whatever gifting they see in you. Ask God to open up avenues or circumstances by which you might exercise your gift, and pray about which of those doors you should open and enter as He pres ents them to you.

Chapter 14

The Greatest Gift of All

"Ye were sealed with that Holy Spirit of promise, which is the earnest of our inheritance." **Eph. 1:13b-14a**

So, of all of the gifts which God rains down upon us, which one is the most important? Which one is the most valuable?

The greatest gift of all, hands down, is the gift of the Holy Spirit.

Why?

For a thousand reasons.

The Holy Spirit is the very Presence of God in us, the heart of what Paul refers to as a "mystery"–"Christ in you, the hope of glory"! He is the carrier by whom every other gift and blessing comes. He is the love of God personified. He is the avenue by which our most humble prayers are conveyed to our Father in Heaven as well as the course by which God responds to our deepest longings. He was the instrument by which we were saved, the voice of God before we knew God existed, the bearer of our forgiveness, the agent of our sanctification, the essence of our righteousness, the power which we possess to bless others, and the guarantee of eternal life. He is God in you, the fullness of the Creator compressed into a personality with whom you can laugh and cry, shout and cheer, sing and dance, walk or run.

As God, the Holy Spirit is free to roam the full expanse of time and space, to play hopscotch among an infinite number of galaxies, and, if He so decides, He could strike out into a new direction by breathing forth more galaxies as well. Yet, with infinite lengths of time and space at His disposal, He has chosen to make His home entirely inside you–your chest, your mind, your hands, your throat, your heart.

He fills you. If you engaged in years and years of therapy and ever so slowly opened the door to the darkest, most shameful lockbox of your soul, you would find Him already in there–knowing everything, grasping the meaning of every passing affect, fully recognizing your misplaced motivations and darkest crimes–and yet LOVING you all the more intensely, all the more completely, all the more richly and extravagantly.

The Holy Spirit is a person. He thinks. He talks. He whispers. He understands. He empathizes. He laughs and cries. He jokes. He always has the right answer. He never demeans, never criticizes, never accuses the believer, never manipulates, never takes unfair advantage. He prizes your tears and delights in your praise. He never forces Himself upon you, never grows impatient, never loses hope, never disregards, never lies or compromises the truth, never abuses or condemns, never acts except in your best interests, never compromises Who He is or Whom He serves or the love that Christ Himself has for you.

He LOVES you. In His Presence is overwhelming 140-proof undiluted joy. He can be as peaceful as the dawn and as rowdy as a midnight honky-tonk. He can be as quiet as baby's breath and as loud as a tornado. He can fill the space around you with an intoxicating fragrance or infuse the air with such power that people pass out simply breathing it. He can tell you things that no one else on Earth has ever known. He can carry you from one place to another without ever crossing the distance in between. He can hide the obvious and reveal the invisible. He can instantaneously give you fluency in new languages. He can empower you beyond human capacity and can disarm all those who oppose you.

He can make you strong. He can make you sensitive. He can make you wise. He has made you righteous. He can make you perfect.

Should I go on?

Let's take a look at the meaning of the verse that opened this chapter. Ephesians 1:13-14 says, ""*Ye were sealed with that Holy Spirit of promise, which is the earnest of our inheritance.*"

"You were sealed" in the same way an ancient king might write a royal decree and then, pressing the design of his royal ring into hot wax, seal the document. The seal tells all inquirers that the document is of royal origin, sent forth for a royal purpose, and carries the full authority of the royal family. You were sealed with the hot wax of the Holy Spirit.

The "promise" is the promise of Christ Himself. Remember when Christ assured His disciples, "It is to your advantage that I go away" because "if I go, I will send Him to you"? (John 16:7) That was His promise. And in Luke's Gospel when Christ, newly risen, says, "Behold, I am sending forth the promise of My Father upon you; but you are to stay in the city until you are clothed with power from on high." (Luke 24:49)

The "earnest" means a "'pledge' or a 'good faith deposit.'" If you've every bought a house, you may have put down a "good faith deposit," meaning some portion of money guaranteeing that the rest of the full purchase price in fact will be delivered. If you fail to deliver, you lose your good faith deposit to the seller. In legal documents, a "good faith deposit" may even be called your "earnest." So the Holy Spirit is the earnest, the good faith deposit representing the bulk of that inheritance which is still promised and set aside in your name.

Understand this: it is a spiritual impossibility that God could ever renege on his promise to you because to do so would make Him a liar. BUT, even if you could begin to imagine that happening, if you could conceive of a circumstance where God would trample underfoot the covenant He made with Abraham and entirely revoke the promises He sealed with the blood of His only biological Son, He would still have to leave His "earnest," His Holy Spirit with you! The Holy Spirit is the earnest, the down payment, and belongs to you already as the very first portion of your divine and physical inheritance.

Note as well, the New Testament was written in Greek. The Greek word Paul used for "earnest" was "arrabon." The modern word "arrabona" is the Greek term for an engagement ring. Once again, by giving us the Holy Spirit as our "arrabon" or pledge, He has represented Himself as the Bridegroom of Promise and us, you and me, as His bride.

Finally, understand this as well. The Holy Spirit is NOT the earnest of your earnings. He is not the down payment on some divine pension plan. You haven't paid in, like Social Security, over the course of your working years so that, in the great hereafter, you can live off of the interest on all of your good deeds. No, No, No! The Holy Spirit is the earnest of our INHERITANCE; a gift inherited, not earned.

I remember when I was six, a skinny asthmatic kid, living on a wooded ridge outside of Pewee Valley, Kentucky. It was a bad time for my dad and a really wretched time for my mom. In three years, my dad would divorce my mom and, in the process, crush everything she was, walking out on her and all seven of us kids.

My mom loved the music of Harry Belafonte, and someone loaned her a copy of "Harry Belafonte at Carnegie Hall." She played that thing until the old stereo needle wore clean through the vinyl and the music poured forth from some miraculous mechanical memory. My mom ironed clothes for hours, listening to Harry Belafonte's wonderful voice echo through the hallowed recesses of Carnegie Hall right into our old Kentucky living room.

My allowance was 25 cents a week, and the record was like $6.50. Each Christmas, I got a dollar, one dollar, to buy gifts for my Mom and six siblings. So $6.50 was a fortune. But I had saved my allowance for months and hoarded every penny. I got my older brother to make the purchase for me, and my sister wrapped it in red paper with a bow.

When my mom unwrapped it, the dimension of my gift stunned her. She didn't think it was real. She couldn't comprehend me saving that much money. And yet here it was. And, to my great joy, she accepted it.

That's what the Holy Spirit is to us! When God reaches the absolute limits of His ability to give to us, the far reaches of His infinite wealth and finds He has no greater gift to give, then He gives us Himself in the form of the Holy Spirit.

The Holy Spirit is the greatest gift of all.

TRUTH:

The Holy Spirit is God's heart, alive and conscious, sown by His design into you.

PRAYER:

My Beloved Father, how absurd it seems too simply say, "Thank You" for a gift so rich that it has to be drawn out of infinite supernatural realms. And yet, Father, it's the only way I know to express my gratitude, to accept with some sense of grace Your lavish blessing. Thank You! Thank You! Thank You! Let me always be grateful! Give me again, Father, the wisdom, the time and the resources to explore this gift –the gift of Your Holy Spirit–throughout all of my days and, in turn, to lavish the measure of Your favor upon all who surround me.

EXERCISE:

When we pray, most of us "talk" to God the Father and to Jesus, failing to recognize that the Holy Spirit is also a living personality and is forever here with us, in us, all around us. Begin a new habit of addressing the Holy Spirit as you open your eyes in the morning. Ask Him about His thoughts regarding you. Ask Him about His feelings, His plans, the things that occupy His mind. You may be surprised at all that He has to say to you.

So What Holds Us Back?

Chapter 15

Poverty of Expectation

"Now unto him that is able to do exceeding abundantly above all that we ask or think, according to the power that worketh in us." **Eph. 3:20**

Twelve words.

Twelve words which loosed the bonds of unbelief and actually equipped me to discover God. Perhaps the most significant words in all of my life, except maybe for that initial prayer of faith recited for the dark-eyed Lebanese woman in Chapter One.

It was October, 2004, and I was the Headmaster of one of the leading non-public schools in Louisiana. At my request, the Board of Directors had resolved that ALL of the school's operating expenses should be covered each year out of tuition revenue–so the number of students we enrolled each fall stood out as a massive issue. We had to have enrollment.

We had about 600 students then, and I decided that, for the next school year, we would storm the gates of Heaven, asking God for 30 more kids. That was a 5% increase, a "reasonable" number in line with the more successful years of our past. To me, 30 more kids seemed right.

Several times a week from October through the following May, June and a very hot July, we prayed for 30 more young people. On Aug. 16, 2005, as we rang the bell to close our first day of the new school year, my angelic secretary Lynn approached me in the front door to my office. With a big smile, she handed me the end-of-day enrollment report. Our enrollment was up exactly 30 kids. We hugged and traded high fives, exclaiming about what we saw as the faithfulness of God.

As I turned away from Lynn and took two steps back into my office, God tazed me. "David," He whispered. Then, in a voice of infinite love and patience, He spoke twelve words that sent me to my knees on the carpet and reduced me to burning tears. ***"Why,"*** He asked, ***"do you confine Me, God, to the poverty of your expectations?"***

Whoa! That would have been enough, but He went on. "You asked me for 30 more students. I've given you that. But you prayed for 30 students because you saw 30 as a 'reasonable' number. So since when am I a reasonable God? Is that the God you want me to be?"

"No, Father! No!" I sobbed. There on the carpet, I repented, thanking Him for His forgiveness and surrendering our enrollment to all that He thought it should be. "God, I'm sorry!" I cried out. "Send us all of the children you think we can serve!"

Twelve days later, Hurricane Katrina roared ashore about 100 miles to the south of us, and the school closed for almost five weeks. By the end of that same year, our enrollment was up more than 140 students. And the following summer, we picked up almost 100 more.

I learned a lesson from that encounter, and I immediately began applying it to every other area of my life. What I learned was this: **unbelief lives within our moment-by-moment expectations.** Unbelief is what seems reasonable in the light of past history and present circumstance. And unbelief is the quickest way to prevent the flow of God's grace and goodness in your life.

How many times in the Scripture did Jesus say, "Let it be done unto you according to your faith"? So what else is "your faith" except the outcome that you anticipate or expect within your immediate circumstances?

Let me give you another example.

A wonderful friend of mine and I drove together one bright and clear

Saturday morning to visit and pray for a man stricken with cancer. As we walked into their country home, his wife Edie was standing awkwardly in the middle of the living room floor, weeping silently. "Oh my gosh, Edie!" we both exclaimed, "what happened?"

"It's fibromyalgia," she cried. "I have a really bad case of fibromyalgia! It feels like some jerk slammed every joint in my body with a ball-peen hammer! It hurts so bad! I can't move. I can't move. I usually control it with medication, but the FDA took my medication off the market, and I can't get the new prescription until Monday."

Immediately, Carter and I layed hands upon her, prayed and spoke to this illness in her body. We prayed for maybe five minutes. When we took our hands off of her, she was well. The pain was gone. She could move freely. She didn't hurt at all. Her fibromyalgia was gone.

"Oh my God!" she exclaimed! "It's gone! It's gone!" She began to move, cautiously at first but then more and more freely until she was hopping around the room, doing deep knee-bends, dancing, and weeping again but, this time, in joy and relief. "Thank you! Thank God!" she cried out and hugged both of us, laughing, weeping and singing all at the same time. Then she said this, "Now I don't have to hurt until I can get my medicine on Monday!!!"

Monday? Monday? Did you get that?

So I ask you, how far did her faith allow her healing to go? Who imposed the limitations? Can you see how her faith–and therefore her healing–was confined, in this case, to the poverty of her expectation?

I tell you this on the basis of dozens of encounters: Edie could have been healed from fibromyalgia COMPLETELY! All she had to do was open her heart and receive it. And yet the poverty of her limited expectations, in effect, threw her absolute healing in the fire, so that she settled for a three-day recess from the pain of her condition.

Edie was victimized by her own unbelief.

After God spoke to me on that August day in 2005, I began to pray every day, "God, set me free from the poverty of my own expectations. Enlarge my heart to believe for the impossible. Tear down every limitation, break up every confining expectation, knock down every false religious teaching, erase the restrictions which my logical mind and personal history attempt to dictate. I don't want God-in-a-box. I want YOU in Your fullness! Be God in my life!"

How does this apply to the day-to-day?

When I travel to teach in Asia, for example, I schedule my time there very loosely. I know what cities I will visit, what days I will teach and preach, and where the believers will gather. I have a loose outline of my teachings in a printed syllabus. Outside of those preparations, I intentionally do NOT set or allow any expectations at all. Then, when God shows up, hundreds of people are healed, prophetic words abound, words of knowledge bubble up everywhere, Hindus and Muslims and idol-worshippers come to Christ, demons are cast out, children see visions, and high schoolers work miracles.

But what about here in the old USA?

Well, God took me out of the job I thought I'd retire from and has given me my own ministry. He has provided for our every financial need including enough that we literally give away thousands of dollars at a time. Our sons have grown in wisdom and grace and become powerful men of faith. I drive someone else's car for free, and we lived in a glorious home for three years where we paid no rent, taxes or fees and even had our grass cut for free. My wife asked me this year what I wanted for Christmas, and, even though we live humbly, I couldn't think of a thing. When a phone call came in last night from a lady seeking to be healed of lymphoma over the phone, my son Sam told me, "Dad, I'm not sure this has ever been said before, but will you please stop working miracles for a long enough time to finish this Scrabble game?"

Poverty of expectation confines most believers to an "average" life, a life of mediocrity, life characterized by very sporadic experiences of

God's power and goodness in their own lives and really no over-flow at all to share with those around them. Their lives play out in gray mediocrity, devoid of the joy and gifting that He holds in His treasury for them.

As I write this book, I think, "If I could instigate one significant change in your life as the reader, what would I want that to be?" And the answer is this: to set you free from the poverty of your expectations.

Please let God deliver you from this crippling poverty.

His entire universe lies before you, His power at your fingertips, His goodness in your hands. Believe! Believe! Believe!

TRUTH:

Unbelief lives within our moment-by-moment expectations. By setting those aside, we open the door for the physical manifestation of God's love and power in the lives of everyone around us.

PRAYER:

Lord Jesus, set me free from the poverty of my own expectations in every area of my life. Break down every confining assumption, every invisible barrier, and be God in my life. Let me believe with every fiber of my being in the goodness of Your character and the grace and liberty You hold here for me. Let me trust You, God. Change my mind and heart to accommodate your supernatural hand. I want you to live and breathe and speak through me.

EXERCISE:

What is it that you ask God to do or be for you? What is the desire of your heart? Scribble down the things that initially come to mind, and then write down what you are actually asking God to accomplish or to give you. Once you have all of those things written down, go back and enlarge every expectation. Go back and change your wish-list from the reasonable to the unreasonable. Go back and ask God to be God in your life.

Chapter 16

Deception:
The Compounding Nature of Lies

"So the great dragon was cast out, that serpent of old, called the Devil and Satan, who deceives the whole world." **Rev. 12:9**

As soon as I met Jessie, I sensed the dark roots behind her ceaseless nervous energy. Well into her autumn years, her light frame skittered around her cluttered living room. Like a restless flock of sparrows, she chattered non-stop, eagerly working to make me comfortable in a house that clearly was not. She pitter-pattered around, straightened books, scolded three yappy poodles, fluffed sofa cushions and re-arranged family photos even as her voice continuously babbled in free-form fashion about a hundred random subjects. The Holy Spirit gave me grace to listen, nod, affirm, comment occasionally, and let this little river run its course. Finally at about the 45-minute mark, she took a deep breath and asked me, "Can I do anything for you?"

"As a matter of fact," I replied and pulled out a straight-back chair, "you can sit down here and let me pray for you."

Cautiously, quietly (!!!) she sat down. I pulled another chair up close, sat, took her hands, and began to talk about God's love for her, listening carefully to her but now letting the Holy Spirit guide the direction of the conversation. I began with the wondrous care that God took in knitting together her substance in the darkness of her mother's womb. We quietly discussed how God had designed her with a purpose in mind, that He might wash and sanctify and claim Jessie for Himself, that she had a future and a hope in Him, and that, in His love, she could find rest. His peace slowly overcame her anxiety. Tears welled and spilled copiously. She prayed with me in a voice of intense longing and absolute surrender to receive His life and blessing. Even the poodles were quiet.

Two days later, Jessie called and asked me to come back. I did. In the same house but now a much different environment, she pulled back the veil and poured forth about her life, how she was born into abject poverty in rural South Dakota, how her step-father brutalized her from the time she was eleven, and how her mother berated her, ordering Jessie to do whatever her stepfather told her as anything else could throw both of them, mother and daughter, into absolute destitution. Jessie talked about running away at 15, a hard early marriage, then finding if not peace at least rest with her second husband, and the joy of their one daughter who–Whoa!–died unexpectedly barely into her twenties.

"Brother Dave," she said, "you need to know that I always felt like God hated me. I was dirty. I was filthy. I've hated mirrors because, no matter how often I looked, all I ever saw there was trash, garbage, a sad girl whose only value was set down there beneath my skirt. For 40 years, Brother Dave, I've changed clothes four, five, six times a day. I've got chests full of underclothes and closets full of soap, skin-wash, shampoo, perfume, alcohol rubs. I've washed six, eight, ten times a day, but none of it ever did me any good."

"When we prayed the other day, something real hard left me. And when I went to sleep last night, I had a dream. I was standing in a big field, all sunlit, peaceful, with flowers blossoming everywhere and a soft breeze blowing. It was beautiful, more beautiful than you could imagine. I could see a path way off in the distance. Two people were walking toward me. One looked human but was made entirely out of light, and I just knew it was Jesus. As they got close, I saw the other was my daughter. She was tall and healthy, smiling. She looked so pretty, Brother Dave, I could hardly breathe. She wore a white dress with little flowers all around the collar. My daughter walked right up to me, looked me dead in the eye, and flashed that pretty smile. Then, real matter-of-fact like, she said, 'Momma, you're finally clean.' Right there, I knew it was true, Brother Dave. I'm different now. He washed me. God Himself has made me clean. I'm clean, Brother Dave. I'm clean."

That conversation happened two years ago now, and Jessie is a much, much different woman. Her husband told me, "Dave, I don't know what happened, but she ain't the woman she used to be."

Understand this: lies and accusation are the language of the enemy. Just as God, just by speaking, caused the entire universe to burst forth out of nothingness, so the enemy crafts his own isolated worlds by building upon spoken words–lie upon lie and accusation upon accusation. The lies of the enemy live on from one generation to the next, on and on and on, building upon one another, seeping the very essence of death and suffering from one generation to the next, to the next, to the next, and so on.

Think of the lies which stole the greater part of Jessie's life. Her step-father had every right to her body, they said. Enduring the bloody pain and torture of it was her responsibility, they said. She received the lie that her value as a human being existed only beneath her skirt, that, outside of that, she was worthless and undesirable. She was, the same voices told her, separate and inferior to other girls and women, an object to be used, regardless of her own pain, for the gratification of whomever could claim even momentary authority over her. Her very nature, she believed, was dirty, despicable, beyond either value or redemption.

But from what convoluted nest did those lies spring? What tangle of darkness excreted the lies which so flooded Jessie's soul year after year? What wretched tangle forged this untruth in the mind of Jessie's mother, that their survival depended upon her throwing her daughter's body on to the altar of her own husband's lust? What kind of dark deception convinced Jessie's stepfather that he had the right to viciously violate Jessie? Were not those lies founded on other lies about God's inability or unwillingness to provide, about the very nature of love, about personal responsibility, even about the existence of God or the value of life at all?

For clarity, let's define as "first generation lies" those which Jessie believed about her own behavior, value and character. Then, understand that the lies which Jessie embraced gushed forth out of a forest of "second-generation" lies perpetrated at some earlier time upon her mother and step-father. No doubt those lies were birthed out of a third generation of falsehoods held by the preceding generation, on and on all the way back to the grandfather of all liars way back in the Garden of Eden.

The enemy revels in lies. He delights in generational dishonesty–deception passed like mothers' milk from one generation to the next over decades, centuries and sometimes even millenia. Deception was the key to his power in the Garden of Eden, and it remains, eons later, the key to his power today. Lies are the very language and nature of the enemy.

How rich then that Christ could step forward and proclaim, "I am the Way, THE TRUTH and the Life!" (John 14:6) And how much joy is there in His proclamation to brand new believers: "If you continue in my word, then you are my disciples indeed; and you shall know the truth, and the truth shall make you free"! (John 8:31-32)

Now grasp this: the brutal strength of the most powerful lies rests in the fact that we often don't recognize them as lies. They're almost invisible, like white noise or seemingly innocuous wallpaper. Yet they possess the power to influence literally EVERYTHING around us.

Even as God spoke to me in 2005 about "the poverty of my expectations," He also began to reveal the lies which I had embraced and which prevented me from knowing Him and loving others effectively. As my eyes were opened, I began praying constantly for Him to reveal and eradicate more and more and more. He holds the power to do that for anyone who asks Him. He is the Truth. And the truth will always set you free.

Here's a starting point. The "flip-side" of this universal law that the truth will set you free is this: if there is ANY area of your life where you are bound up, prone to stress or terror or rage, overly sensitive to the remarks or actions of others, the cause of your discomfort is almost always centered in some untruth, some lie, some form of deception which you've unwittingly embraced.

Know this: Christ is the Truth. He can set you free.

The truth will always, always, always set you free.

TRUTH:

Whenever we are emotionally bound up and prone to physical stress, the root cause rests in the fact that we have unwittingly embraced some untruth. By supplanting that lie with God's truth, we rediscover freedom.

PRAYER:

Lord Jesus, I recognize and confess that deception is the birthing-ground of fear and anger, hatred and self-righteousness, anxiety, suffering and pain. I ask You, Father, set me free. Identify the lies in my own life, the untruth which I have unknowingly embraced, the dishonesty that was ingested probably from the moment of my birth. Lord Jesus, you promised the Holy Spirit would guide me into all truth. Those are Your words, Your promises. Make this true in my life, Father. Eradicate every form and foundation of deception in my life. I ask You, Father, set me free.

EXERCISE:

Take time to examine the stresses and fears which are common in your life. Ask God to reveal those to you. Speak them out loud as He presents them to your mind. Hand those over to Him, even physically holding out your hands and allowing Him to lift them out of your arms. Listen to the Holy Spirit as He whispers into your heart God's corresponding truth. Search the Scripture for His promises and teaching on the truth which He speaks to you, and arm yourself against the falsehood you once believed by memorizing Scripture which draws you into healing and rest. Ask Him to make you sensitive to those moments when you are tempted to slide back into unbelief, and, in those moments, consciously choose to stand and act in accordance with his healing word.

Chapter 17

Accusation:
The Voice of Your Enemy

"The accuser of our brethren has been thrown down, he who accuses
them before our God day and night" **Rev. 12:10**

The first exorcism I ever experienced happened in Agra, India.

It was July, the monsoon season, and hotter than humans ever want to experience. The air was so humid that the old air conditioner in our hotel caused water to condense every night on the walls and, dripping down, to pool on the floor. Every morning, my son Sam and I woke up suspended above a shallow ocean, a quarter-inch of liquid stretching from base-board to base-board.

Our "doorbell" screamed like a wounded cat about 11:45 one night, and Sam, answering it, told me pastors were asking me to come right away to room 106. Approaching that door, I could hear yelling inside. A glance at my watch told me it was straight-up midnight.

The demoniac was one of our translators. He lay spread-eagle on a mattress, four grown men holding him down. The room was a wreck, covers and furniture strewn everywhere and crowded with eight pastors. For three hours, "Martin" screamed and cursed, wailed, growled, laughed at and mocked us, sang hymns and cursed God, fought us and, if he got an arm free, threw at us whatever he could grab. At least six demons left Martin, but, by the end, he was free. It was a long, drawn out battle.

In the middle of this melee, our mission leader sent for two young pastors as reinforcements. Like me, this was new territory for them, and they came in eager for battle, confident, ready to confront the legions of Hell if such a demonic army chose to present itself.

As soon as they entered, the demon began laughing derisively. Then, for five minutes, the demon-of-the-moment vomited out all these pastors' darkest fantasies, their most shameful sins. He ACCUSED them. He spread out their sins for the rest of us like a jig-saw puzzle. Dismay blossomed forth upon their faces. Confidence drained away like bathwater. As soon as a convenient moment surfaced, they both quietly and meekly bowed out and evacuated.

This is truth: you will never experience lasting peace with God until you understand that He has forgiven ALL of your sins and declared you to be absolutely righteous.

For years, I used to go to church largely to be accused. I loved "conviction." I wanted the pastor to "step all over my toes." I honestly believed that I'd been short-changed at church if the preacher didn't make me feel that I was a worthless sinner, created to tremble before a holy, righteous and probably very angry God.

Now I know that kind of preaching is sick. It's perverted. It's a denial of God's love and goodness toward me. It's unbelief. It's a perspective for spiritual cripples, "still-born again," in danger of enduring the rest of their lives like beaten dogs cowering before a sour-faced master when the true Master gave His Son's lifeblood in order to lavish His goodness upon them. Theirs is not Godliness. It is not holiness. It is deception, false teaching and a gross misunderstanding of the Scripture. I won't go there again.

In the early church, even brand new believers were expected to understand this truth. John writes, "I am writing to you, little children (meaning the very newest of those who had trusted in Christ), because your sins have been forgiven you for His name's sake." (1 John 2:12) The author of Hebrews rebukes his readers, calling them spiritual "babies" because they have not come to understand the "doctrine of righteousness." (Hebrews 5:11-13)

Understand this: when you embrace the truth of your own righteousness and begin to walk every day in the realization of your God-given innocence, two things are sure to happen.

The first is that well-intentioned believers will accuse you of being spiritually boastful and a victim of heretical teaching. They will point at verses like 1 John 1:8-10, Romans 7, 1 Timothy 1:15 and even the Lord's Prayer. They are wrong. While this is not the time to mount a point-by-point defense of God's truth, the whole of Scripture, correctly interpreted, is entirely on your side.

The second is that you will see the intimacy of your time with the Savior blossom in dimensions you never thought possible. You will understand for the first time the meaning of freedom. You will begin to experience His gifting and power as you never have before. You will know the truth, and the truth will set you free. (John 8:32)

David Samuel, an Indian minister and perhaps the wisest Christian man I ever met, constantly tells me that Americans don't have a clue about the power that lies within a proper understanding of forgiveness. More and more, I understand David's perspective.

Very recently, I engaged in another exorcism, this time over two days with a woman molested and then "married" to a demon in a Satanic ritual. The demon plagued her for years, audibly and sexually threatening her children who were as young as four, and degrading this woman in every form and fashion until her health broke down completely.

The anchor that this demonic power had found in Sheila's mind and heart was NOT any of the various sins in which she engaged and he delighted. The sins themselves were NOT the substance of his stronghold. His anchor lay instead in the fact that she could not forgive herself. Because she received and believed his unrelenting accusation, she could not experience the inheritance of righteousness which God Himself continuously and freely offered her.

In the midst of her exorcism, the demon would take control of her body and mind, mocking and cursing at us. I would call her up to the surface and ask her to assume authority. "Shiela! Shiela!" I told her over and over again. "You can do this. Take control and talk to me." The defiant angry eyes of the demonic power would subside, and I would see her plaintive and exhausted soul reflected there. "Now," I told her, "repeat after me! Tell this demon, "I forgive myself! I forgive myself! God has forgiven me, and I forgive myself!""

Finally, when she could speak forth those words, her body stiffened, her back arched over the arm of the sofa where she sat, her feet scraped on the floor, her neck was taut and twisted. An unearthly groan emerged from her clenched teeth, and she cried out, "I forgive myself!" After perhaps 45 seconds of this painful contortion, the demon left her. To the best of my knowledge, she is still free.

Satan is the "accuser of the brethren...which accused them before our God day and night." (Rev. 12:10) In my deluded religious years, I used to think Rev. 12:10 depicted a situation in which Satan continuously and vehemently spoke to God about all of my sins and failures. It took years to realize Satan wasn't talking to God. Satan was talking to me. He speaks to us. Satan's accusing voice is directed at us. He "accuses the brethren."

Why? Because, if he can prevent us from grasping our unassailable righteousness, then he can nail our feet to a position of weakness and spiritual immaturity. He can tether us to the cross and rob us of our personal experience of the resurrection. In this earthly life, he can deny us our access to the peace and power which is our inheritance in Christ. He can neutralize us as soldiers of the cross just as he did those two young Indian pastors.

Don't let him do that.

It's up to you to receive the totality of God's forgiveness and, in doing so, step into a position of inheritance and power. (Romans 5:17)

Claim, embrace and know the gift of righteousness which Christ has given to ALL who trust in Him. Honor Him by receiving it afresh, believing it, reminding yourself of it on a daily basis. You can walk (as Noah did) continuously—moment by moment by moment—in that "righteousness which is by faith"!

TRUTH:

The devil's power lies in His ability to convince you of your own unworthiness, causing you to deny the value of Christ's sacrifice on your behalf and the corresponding gift of righteousness which is yours in Him.

PRAYER:

Father in Heaven, I don't want to camp out in the foyer! I don't want to live a life of spiritual poverty and limitation! I don't want the enemy to deny me the fullness of Your calling, the truth of all that I can be in You! I embrace the reality of all that You have done for me. I accept and confirm and thank You for the gift of Your–not "my" but 'Your"–absolute righteousness. I beg you, Father, make the truth of that righteousness illuminate the darkest, most closely guarded areas of my life. Let the wind of your Presence sweep in like the first storms of spring. Drive out every shadow of accusation in my life, and refresh me with the certain truth of your acceptance and approval. I need this, God. I need You.

EXERCISE:

Do you understand that God's gift of righteousness covers every area of your life? By His power, you are not only cleansed and declared holy, but, by embracing that truth, you are led into a daily walk that reflects His nature, His character, His spotless life. When you stumble in an area of recurring ungodliness, instead of shamedly asking His forgiveness again, THANK Him for the righteousness which He has already credited to your account. Then walk as a rich man walks, in the confidence of knowing that which you possess.

Chapter 18

Dad

"Our Father who art in Heaven..." **Matt. 6:9**

I love the story about a kindergartner who was diligently concentrating on a drawing at her desk. The teacher was astounded by the little girl's intensity and asked her, "Zoe, what in the world are you drawing?"

"God," said Zoe, very matter-of-factly. "I'm drawing God."

"Oh, baby," said the teacher, "nobody in the whole wide world knows what God looks like!"

"Well," said Zoe, "they will in a minute."

The truth is that all of us have some image of God from the time that we are very small; a larger truth is that He always looks a lot like our dads. It is in our very nature that, until we mature in faith, our image of God and our image of our dads are inextricably connected and alike.

It takes about nine nano-seconds to discern that this phenomenon presents a world of problems. While there are definite blessings involved, our situation is a lot like that of an amateur beekeeper; we know there's a treasure trove of honey in there somewhere, but, if we don't approach the situation with faith and clarity, we get stung every time.

What's that mean?

It means, if you had an absent dad, you probably carry around a lot of anxieties about God simply not being there when you need Him.

If you had a workaholic dad, then you're likely to act out of the assumption that you really don't matter enough to God, that surely He's busy juggling far more pressing needs than yours, that your concerns are not important to Him. He's distracted even when He says, "I love you."

If you had a demanding and punitive dad, then you probably have a lot of ingrained heart-issues which you have to overcome even to begin to understand that you walk always, as a believer, in the unconditional acceptance and full unassailable approval of your Heavenly Father.

If your dad was prone to cyclones of fear or rage, then you might see God the same way–uncertain, preoccupied, angry or potentially violent.

Until we come into a meaningful relationship with the Holy Spirit, God always looks like dad, sharing the same characteristics, the same question marks that clothed our dear old dads.

My dad was the very best and absolute worst man I ever knew.

On the one hand, his gifts were legend. He was a brilliant physician with an astounding photographic memory for everything he ever read and every person he ever met. Someone might ask him a question about some exotic illness native to only certain tribes of Zambia, and, if he had read an article about it 20 years before, he could pull it up in his mind and read you the text from this photographic image in his head. In the same way, he could meet a patient once, not see him again for 20 years, and, when he or she crossed his path the second time, my dad would re-member the patient's name and something about the family. It was scary.

At 6'4" with a massive 60-inch chest, he dominated large spaces. He was handsome and a good conversationalist. Women fell in love with him in minutes–a very mixed blessing–and men bragged about his friendship. He made house calls on a Harley, flew planes as well as Chuck Yeager, and owned a boat big enough to host a real fishing party.

But my dad was also horrendously abused as a child by his dad, and, out of that, he saw himself as entirely unlovable. He drank a fifth of Wild Turkey every day sometimes for months at a time. He binge smoked. He ran around on all of his four wives. He was abusive to those who most loved him, challenging them to constantly prove their love for him. And as careful as he was of the lives of his patients, he was ab-solutely reckless with his own. He once forced my mother, who loved him without limits, to watch him play Russian roulette, spinning the wheel on a loaded pistol, pressing it to his temple, counting slowly to three, and pulling the trigger without either one of them knowing whether the one bullet in the gun was in the chamber or not.

When he divorced my mom, he crushed her–slowly, incrementally and completely. And when he walked out of the lives of myself and my six siblings, he apparently didn't look back. No fight for visitation rights. No custody issues. He just picked up his medical bag and walked away...

...in every form but financially. He was always there for us financially. He paid all of our tuition from kindergarten through college and placed very few limitations on the details of our weddings. We had nice cars, a beautiful family home on nine-acres of river-front property, landscaped with azaleas, camellias, and massive pine trees. He was always there to replace the water pump, the clothes dryer, the dishwasher, or to finance almost any dream we could coherently present to him.

So guess what.

For years, I held on to two fears in my understanding of God.

The first fear was that He would simply one day abandon me, that He would pick up His bag for no apparent reason and walk out of my life.

The second, oddly enough, was financial. I feared that somehow God would not meet my needs, would not be there for me financially when I needed Him the most. On the surface, that's an odd thing, because financial provision was the one area where my earthly dad was attentive and generous, but the issue with "Doc" was that we always had to ask him. Given his volatile nature, that in itself could be a chore. You kind of had to plan carefully and crawl a little bit as if to assuage his guilt for every other failing. And the outcome, though consistently favorable, was never ever certain. My oldest brother nicknamed him "Screaming Jack" out of the meetings surrounding our financial needs.

So I transferred the attributes of my earthly father, "Doc," to my understanding of my Heavenly Father. Because of my earthly dad's personality, I saw God as removed, non-communicative, better read about than actually engaged, all-knowing but erratic, intentionally cruel but also potentially generous if I worshipped Him with sufficient vigor and intensity.

That image was a lousy substitute for the God whom I now know.

So what legacy has your earthly father left you? What false impression, what wrongful characterization, what undeserved limitation have you embraced about God because of the all-too-human limitations of the man you knew or should have known as "dad"?

I started this chapter with the story of Zoe drawing her picture of God. Out of that picture, you need to understand two truths.

First, God may not look like your dad. Don't hold either one of them to the burdens of that comparison. Don't let your dad's limitations constrict your perception of God, and don't hold your own dad responsible for the flaws and faults which become abundantly clear in light of what God really looks like. Nobody ought to have to stand next to God for comparison purposes. Know your father's faults, but divorce him from the consequences of those same shortcomings in your life. Extend to him the grace and forgiveness which God Himself, at His own great expense, has lavished upon you. Your dad deserves that, no matter who he is.

Second, understand the wisdom of Zoe. Like Zoe, God Himself, day by day, is drawing His own picture, fashioning you into the express image of His person, coloring His image of you daily with the goodness and glory of His own Person. The Creator of Heaven and Earth is redrawing you as a picture of Himself for a purpose: to present Himself through you to everyone else you know. "Put on the new man," says Paul in Ephesians 4:24, "which in the likeness of God has been created in righteousness and holiness of the truth."

The world around us does not know what God looks like.

We have the opportunity to show them.

TRUTH:

God doesn't look like your dad. Set both of them free from the weight of that comparison.

PRAYER:

Father, I want to know You in your fullness. I ask You, Heavenly Father, to remove every constraint from my understanding of who You are and how You love me. Release my own father from the consequences of his failures and shortcomings in my life, and reveal Yourself to me as my Heavenly Father. Show me Your glory, God. I want to know You as the ultimate Father. Show me your glory. Mark me forever, as You transformed the very face of Moses. Make me as one who knows Your glory.

EXERCISE:

Write a letter to your dad, thanking him for the role he played in your life. In the process of writing that letter, set aside every form of bitterness or resentment you might have harbored toward your dad, and let him know that he walks in the grace of God's forgiveness in your life. Release him as well from every expectation, every debt your heart has told you that he owes you. If there are any outstanding debts which you owe him, tell him that you want to make good on those–and then follow through. Show your own dad the limitless, undeserved love of Christ. I promise that, if your letter shows forth the grace of God, healing will manifest in both of you.

Chapter 19

The Cost of Unforgiveness

"Forgive us our trespasses..." Matt. 6:12

Do you realize how many people recite The Lord's Prayer without ever stopping to consider what they're saying? Hundreds of millions! So look at this line from the most common English translation: ***"Forgive us our trespasses as we forgive those who trespass against us."***

Now let me ask this: do you really want God to forgive your sins only to the degree that you forgive people who have sinned against you? Hello? "Forgive me my trespasses" is cool, but do I really want to limit God's forgiveness in my life to this standard–"as I forgive those who trespass against me"? Read it again! Is that not what it seems to say?

I consider myself a forgiving person, but, I confess, in the weakness of my flesh, I'm not above occasionally wishing God would pour out a little Old Testament justice on some offending goon. Do I really want Him to forgive me "as I forgive those who trespass against me"?

What does that prayer actually mean?

If you really pore over the Greek, I think you'll find Jesus' intent could be more accurately translated like this: "Release me from, separate me from, (literally) divorce me from the consequences of my sins even as I learn to do the same for those who have sinned against me."

Let me give you the best example I know.

I've already told you about my dad, about his being both the best and worst person I've ever known. What I won't detail is the emotional havoc that he inflicted on others, primarily his wives and children, whose only sin was to love him deeply. Leave it at this: it was horrifying.

For years then, Debbie and I prayed that we could introduce my dad to Christ. We wanted to see him set free. On our occasional visits, we would leap at opportunities to speak of God's grace or favor in our lives. Almost every time, he would hear us and engage momentarily. Then as we rose to the bait, as soon as we perceived some illusory chance to have a meaningful conversation about Christ, he would–WHAM!–lash out at us with obscene ferocity so that it felt as if we'd been physically assaulted, bludgeoned in exchange for our prayers and concern.

So on a peaceful morning one weekend, I asked Doc out of the blue to tell me the story of his and my mom's divorce. I was truly curious as to what he would say and, perhaps unconsciously at first, I yearned to hear some iota of remorse, some passing remembrance of regret over his abandoning my mom, myself and my six siblings so many years before.

Suffice it to say that he related the most self-serving, ludicrous saga, an accusatory fairy tale which I knew to be absurdly inaccurate. I said nothing. At the end, however, I knew that the conversation had become something hugely important to me. Suddenly deeply conscious of my own aching need, I handed him a golden opportunity. "So, Doc," I asked him, "if you had the chance to live those years all over again, what would you do differently?" In my eyes, this was the opportunity of a lifetime, the perfect occasion for him to simply utter some healing word, to reach out across so many years of his absence and let me know that, yes, he knew the pain, the aching void he'd caused and, if not sorry, would at least value the opportunity of the moment.

For perhaps 60 silent seconds, I could see his lightning-quick mind explore possible answers, weighing costs and potential benefits. Then, with absolutely emotionless clarity, he said, "I wouldn't change a thing."

All the pain I had experienced for as long as I could remember welled up, and, deep inside, I felt this tsunami of anger swelling along the ocean floor but moving up toward the surface. Sitting at his breakfast table, I consciously thought of the knife lying on the counter right behind me. Even now, I believe murder would have been completely justifiable.

Then I felt the Holy Spirit still my mind and quietly redirect my course. Almost without thought at all, I said, "Okay, Doc, now it's my turn." He looked up with some surprise. "I want you to hear this really clearly," I said. "I want my words to sink in so deep that they'll ring in your ears every day until the very day you die."

Whoa! He set down whatever he was holding and looked at me, unapologetic but bracing himself in case I tried to bludgeon him in return.

"Doc, I want you to go way back again," I said. "Like a slide show, I want you to glimpse every decision, every choice you've ever made which may have affected our relationship directly or indirectly since before I was first conceived." I paused and then asked, "You got that?"

"I think so."

"Good," I continued. "Now from this moment, let your mind speculate on the endless possibilities that rest in every moment of the future. Doc, I could stand up right now and hug you. I could also grab that knife on the counter behind me and cut your throat. We could retire one day and spend a lot of days fishing for bass at Toledo Bend, or you could go mad and kill my wife and sons. EVERY possibility exists. I've accounted for all of them. Do you understand that?"

"I do," he said.

"Then hear this, Doc, and remember it," I said. I leaned forward, locked eyes with him, and spoke very slowly and distinctly. "I. Will. Always. Love. You. Do you hear me?"

"Yes." He averted his eyes, and I continued.

"I will always love you. There's nothing you can ever do about that. It's a decision I've made regardless of any action or inaction on your part. You can't divorce yourself from that. You can't get away from it. If you murder my sons, I will love you. If you steal everything I own and brutalize me to the point of madness, I will love you. The past doesn't count any more. The present's not important. And the future will never change this. I will always love you. You're my dad. I will always love you."

From that day, a new dawn rose up in my relationship with my dad. He began occasionally to confide in me some of his deeper fears and regrets. Our conversation took on a peaceful assurance which had not been there before. I still grabbed most opportunities to share Christ's importance in my life, but his obscene and blasphemous rejoinders grew less frequent and finally ceased altogether.

A few weeks before he died, I drove him to see his opthalmologist. We ended up in the darkest room I've ever experienced. The doctor medicated my dad's eyes to dilate his pupils and then shut us in this black room to allow time for the medicine to work. We sat there for long minutes, each of us absolutely quiet. then like a lone lightning bolt on a dark, dark night, his voice broke the stillness.

"You need to know this: I accepted Christ six weeks ago," he said.

"What?"

"I accepted Christ six weeks ago," he repeated. "I walked the aisle at First Baptist Church in Long Beach, Mississippi, and prayed to receive Christ with Pastor Jimmy there at the front of the church."

"That's great, Doc," I said. "Why didn't you tell me earlier?"

"I figured, if it was real, you'd see a difference."

And I did. I saw a lot over the declining months of his life, and I'm thankful for both the grace of God and for the dad He gave me. We released one another from the consequences of our own sins, and we both were transformed by it. I'm still looking forward to fishing together.

I believe that's what Jesus meant when He encouraged us to "pray after this manner" and, then, in the midst of his short lesson, said, "Forgive us our trespasses as we forgive those who trespass against us." In other words, "Divorce me from the consequences of my own sins even as I learn to do the same for those who have sinned against me."

Forgiveness is a powerful thing.

TRUTH:

There is more reward in bringing life to someone than there is in wishing harm to them.

PRAYER:

Father, teach me to forgive others even as You have forgiven me. Teach me, Lord, the value of forgiveness.

EXERCISE:

Ask God to reveal to you the people in your life against whom you hold some animosity, some regret, some measure of bitterness or hurt. Write their names down. Then read the next chapter.

Chapter 20

The Power of Forgiveness

"...even as we forgive those who trespass against us" Matt. 6:12

The first time I recognized that David Samuel was a force to be reckoned with, we were teaching in a church about 40 miles from the India-Pakistan border. The church service was winding to a close, and lots of people were lingering there, wiry men asking me to pray for them, shy women wanting me to bless little bottles of anointing oil, teenagers wanting to pose with me for "just one click, please, sir."

A dark-skinned young man came in and urgently grabbed David's arm. "Please come, sir. Please come. My mother needs prayer," he pleaded. David pointed out that he was effectively in charge of my teaching service, but the man was not to be dissuaded. "Sir, the service is over. They don't need you here. My mother is dying, and she is resting only two blocks away. You must come now, sir. Now, sir. Please, sir." David relented, told me he'd be back, and followed the little man out.

The man's mother was enduring the final stages of lung cancer. She was desperately weak, gaunt, her skin gray, and her lungs so full of cancer that she could not lift her elbows without overwhelming pain. Her breath fluttered and wheezed. David sat on the floor next to her woven sleeping mat and gently began to talk with her. He was respectful, compassionate, not prone to touch but not hesitant either, asking her simple "yes" and "no" questions so as not to tax what little breath she could manage. They talked and prayed quietly. She had been Hindu all of her life, but she had no trouble embracing Christ, repeating the simplest of acknowledgements word for word as David spoke them for her.

The conversation continued, the Spirit now clearly involved and the woman hanging on David's every word. She had questions; he had answers. She laughed very briefly, and they prayed again, this time speaking out forgiveness of specific people who had offended her or whom she disliked. She and David talked more until she lost sight of her own illness and was simply wrapped up in the freedom, joy and peace that flowed all around her. Altogether, maybe 90 minutes had slipped by.

"Now," David said to her, his voice a whisper, "lift your arms."

She did. Easily. Freely. With no pain or constriction.

Her cancer was gone.

Her lungs were clear.

She got up and, that night, helped prepare dinner for her family.

The next day, she walked to church with her whole family. She was thin but strong, not gray-skinned but full of life, sure-footed and confident, overjoyed and ready to learn more about this Christ who had so clearly touched and healed her. Right there in the church, I got to hear her story directly.

It is David who tells me often, "My brother, Americans have no understanding at all about the power of forgiveness."

He's right. And I am American, but I'm learning.

What I do know is this.

Unforgiveness always involves at least two parties. One is the angry victim, and the other is the targeted perpetrator. The angry person may have good cause for rage, a legitimate bone to gnaw upon, may have suffered some significant wound or huge loss because of the perpetrator's offending word or deed. The offense may have been entirely intentional, premeditated, completely inexcusable and impossible for the guilty party to honestly deny. The wounded party may be entirely right.

But what I also know is that, almost always, the wounded party suffers most because of his or her unforgiveness. Very often, the guilty party holds little or no knowledge of the offense or has justified his actions and moved on to the point of forgetfulness. The perpetrator is guilty but free, while the victim, presumably innocent, is suffering and an easy target for a host of malicious powers and afflictions.

As I've learned more about healing, I've watched people instantly set free from spinal pain, stomach troubles and blinding headaches. I've seen scoliosis healed, cancer healed, fibromyalgia healed, crohn's disease and ulcers and heart disease healed, and loads of painful back conditions healed–all in part as a function of the sick person's ability to lay down offenses and forgive those who have wronged him.

I've learned that holding on to unforgiveness is slow poison. It binds and cripples, twists and constricts, strangles, tortures and eventually kills. It does all that NOT to the perpetrator but to the victim, the one who suffered the initial complaint, who has now embraced rage and resentment. Unforgiveness is deception in its most subtle and self-serving form, and it is absolutely poisonous.

A woman, close to me, was once the victim of a violent crime. In the midst of that violence, she suddenly recovered memories of her own father molesting her more than 30 years before. The memories were very vivid, specific to a single verifiable time and place. Her father was of such a character that very few people doubted the veracity of her remembrance, and the shame and trauma of that recovered memory sent her whole life into a tailspin. Shock settled into hurt. Hurt swelled into anger. Anger simmered into bitterness. Bitterness flamed into rage. And rage smoldered in a dark cloud of unforgiveness.

The crime became such a central issue to her life that she could think of little else. Her work suffered, Her friendships suffered. Her family relationships suffered. Her dad, now old and infirmed, knew nothing of her situation, nothing of her mindset, nothing of the long-buried trauma that had now blossomed into a massive stinkweed in her life.

"I'm going to confront him," she told me. "I'm driving there now. I need to let that bastard know what he did to me, the havoc he's unleashed in my life. I need to tell him face-to-face, eye-to-eye. I want to see his shock and pain."

"What if it kills him?" I asked. "Will that satisfy you?"

"I don't know," she said, "but I don't want that pathetic excuse of a man to go to his grave thinking it's all okay, that I'm still his lovely daughter, that I haven't been through the hell he's wrought in my life."

"And then what?" I asked.

"You don't get it, Jackie," I told her. "The only way out for you is to forgive him, to pull the whole thing out of your heart like a dark and poisonous root, to hold it up in the light and let God take it from you. You need to give it to Him, acknowledge that He's nailed it to the cross, and get on with the rest of your life. Even if you hate your dad, Jackie, this doesn't work. As long as you hold on to the hurt, he wins. And when he dies, he's free, and you're not. You're left here nursing off of a cadaver, sucking death out of a body that should have been embalmed and buried long, long ago."

Here's the truth. Most people, when asked about the issues of unforgiveness in their lives, can actually point to the places in their bodies where the stress associated with that offense is stored in their muscles, the bone structure or their internal organs. Once they connect the dots between the physical and spiritual, they can feel and identify the related repositories of tension and stress in their bodies. Ask any doctor about this: stress, unrelieved over a long period of time, wreaks havoc on the body. It's a simple medical truth.

In the same way, Jesus doesn't tell you to forgive your enemies in any way to benefit your enemies. He tells you to forgive your enemies for YOUR benefit, because releasing others first releases you. Forgiving others sets you free. It frees you and strengthens you. It allows your body to heal and your heart to hear God more clearly.

Forgiveness sets you free.

TRUTH:

Forgiving others sets us free.

PRAYER:

Father, as I consider in this very moment the various people in my life who have offended or wounded me, people against whom I hold some smoldering anger or fear, I lift them up and hand them to You. You, Father, have said, "Come unto Me, all you who are burdened and heavy-laden, and I will give you rest." Those are Your words, Father, not mine. Those are Your words, and I choose now to stand upon the truth of that word. Free me from unforgiveness. Identify and remove every form of resentment or bitterness, anger or fear from my soul and body. Free me, and teach me in the process to free others. Free me, Father. Set me free.

EXERCISE:

Ask God to reveal to you the name of any person against whom you hold any form of anger or resentment. As he brings those to mind, write them down on a sheet of paper. When no more seem to rise up in your mind, go down your list and, out loud, release each one from whatever violence or difficulty they introduced into your life. Speak your forgiveness out loud as an act of obedience and a declaration of your own emerging freedom. As you speak their name and their offense, be aware of the places in your body where you have deposited, held on to and nursed your anger and resentment. Consciously release that stress, reaching with your hand or hands to that spot, grasping the hurt and pulling it out and away from your body.

When you've exhausted the list and cast every form of bitterness away from your mind and body, burn the list and let all of the bitterness you've felt burn up in the flame. Then rest. Rest and let God fill the newly empty spots in your heart with His healing Presence. Rest in the fullness of His forgiveness and care.

I'd love it if you sent me a report on how this made you feel and the healing that God brings you. You can find e-mail me at dave@davedia-mond.net. I'd love to hear from you.

Chapter 21

The Lifeless Path of Religion

"But he that is joined to the Lord is one spirit." 1 Cor. 6:17

It's easy to make a whipping boy out of "church." It's so easy to focus on the negatives of our common church experience that even really great churches end up looking like the nerd in everybody's fifth grade class; he's just an easy target. But, in the end, what's the point?

I've been Roman Catholic, Southern Baptist, and belonged to an Evangelical Free Bible Church. I've worshipped in Assemblies of God, Churches of God, Presbyterian, Lutheran and Episcopalian churches. I've ministered to Mormons and Jehovah's Witnesses. Regardless of religious flavor, most people are involved in a legitimate search for that which is real and meaningful, a quest for some certainty of God's favor which they can then translate into the hurly-burly of every day life.

Luke's Gospel tells us that, on the night Christ was born, resplendent angels filled the sky, crying out, "On Earth, peace! Good will toward men!" (Luke 2:13-14) Wise men came to Bethlehem in search of that very thing. Millions of other wise men have pursued the same elusive reward, the same assurance of God's compassionate favor. Most organized religions offer some path by which earlier generations achieved some grasp of this blessed existence; isn't that the means of their attraction?

By His grace, I've discovered two truths that most churches miss.

First, I don't have to search for peace with God, for divine favor, for the dizzying realization that He has embraced me fully and legally as His own. It is mine, once again, by inheritance. All I have to do is receive it. Romans 5:17 reads like this: "Those who RECEIVE of the abundance of grace and of the gift of righteousness will REIGN in life by one Christ Jesus." We simply receive.

The second secret is this: I take Him at His Word. While I am not dependent upon the Bible for my life in Christ, I can step out upon the authority of what is written there. I love Scripture. I study Scripture carefully to try to discern God's intent. I compare Scripture to Scripture, examine translations, research vocabulary, sort through tenses and sentence structure, explore context, dig to understand author and audience. Then I listen to the Holy Spirit, inviting Him to show me the truth at hand and how that particular fragment meshes with God's larger truth. Religious people, on the other hand, often swear by Scripture but don't believe it; they make excuses for God to maintain illusions of righteousness or relationship in spite of the poverty of their personal experience.

The biggest problem we should all have with religion was best encapsulated by a huge billboard I used to pass on my way to work. In bold-faced script plastered on the side of this church was the name of the church and then this braggadocios phrase: "Striving to Be Like Christ!"

Whoa! Can you see the poison in that prescription? To me, "Striving to Be Like Christ" is the essence of religion. In true faith, there is no striving. "Striving" means "exerting oneself vigorously; working hard; struggling vigorously; or contending in opposition, battle or conflict." Doesn't sound like "receiving" to me. Sounds like "exhaustion."

But the bigger problem lies with this phrase: "to be like Christ."

I don't ever want "to be like Christ."

Understand this: I want to be Christ.

"Like" involves "similarity." What God offers is not similarity; it's unity. It's not intimacy; it's unity. It's not fellowship; it's unity. Between Jesus and me, it's unity. I don't want "to be like"; I want "to be."

To speak of "Striving to Be Like Christ" is attractive because we find satisfaction in being similar, alike, comparable, akin, or even identical. But all of those terms imply duality. To be similar, you are necessarily two. To be alike or comparable, you are necessarily two. To resemble someone, you are necessarily two. What God offers us is one-ness.

Knowing that identity is a function of our spirit, look at 1 Cor. 6:17: "He that is joined to the Lord is ONE SPIRIT." We have one spirit with Him, one identity. Religion promotes similarity, likeness, resemblance or parallelism. Christ offers one-ness, singularity, wholeness in Him.

Understand what I am saying and not saying. I am NOT God Who spoke the universe into being. I am NOT Jesus who was born of Mary and went to the cross for me. BUT, by His grace, the risen Christ has chosen to invest Himself into my physical body and has so fused His identity with mine that we are–by His Word, not mine–one spirit. My body is His chosen means by which He manifests and displays His life to other men. I am, by faith, so possessed by the Spirit of God that His thoughts become my thoughts, my hands become His hands, His voice becomes my voice. We are inextricably united. We are one.

I am NOT the totality of God. If you lost a hand in an accident and a policeman picked it up on the side of the road, he wouldn't exclaim, "Hey! I found Bob!" But at the same time, your hand is you–a part of you, an instrument of expression, a tool through which you share and relate. In the same way, you are Christ. And the more you comprehend your one-ness with Him, the easier it is to express His Presence to others.

To say, "I am Christ" upsets religious people. But the danger lies not in thinking, "I am Christ." The danger lies in denying that one-ness, the fullness of His Presence in us. When we constrain and limit that irrevocable unity, we limit His ability to work inside and to express Himself through us. Think. He said we would do greater works than He did (John 14:12), that ANYTHING we ask is possible (Matt. 17:20), that He has invested into us the power to literally move mountains (Matt. 17:20), that, so far, we "have asked nothing" (John 16:24)! In us, He has ALL authority. We are one. "As He is, so are we in the world"! (1 John 4:17)

Within that context, four smaller lies define false religion.

First is "distance," the teaching that we as believers are somehow separated from God. Distance is simply the continuation of duality, casting you and God as separate beings, two instead of one. There is no distance between you and God. You can't divide one and still be one.

The second is "demand," that there is something that I must do to achieve or maintain one-ness. The New Testament is not about "demand." It's about supply. It's not striving; it's receiving. It's not earning; it's inheritance. Even our obedience is a function of God in us. Ezekiel the Prophet wrote, "Thus saith the Lord...'I will...cause you to walk in my statutes, and ye shall keep my judgments, and do them.'" (Ezek. 36:22,27)

The third lie is "delay," that we enter God's Kingdom when we die. In all four Gospels, Jesus began His ministry by preaching, "The Kingdom of Heaven is at hand!" The Kingdom is present, palpable, accessible NOW–NOW!–to those who believe. There is no delay.

And the fourth lie is "denial," that God has not ALREADY blessed you with every spiritual blessing (Eph. 1:3), that somehow He arbitrarily withholds blessings from His children. The Christ I know says, "Fear not, little flock! It is your Father's good pleasure to give you the Kingdom!" (Luke 12:32) The Kingdom, mind you! Not some tinkertoy bauble. There's no camping out in the foyer! It's the whole Kingdom!

There is no life in duality, no joy in false religion.

We are one with Him. We are His body. He gives us one-ness. False religion teaches duality. True faith confers one-ness–absolute peace, unity, good will, complete and total identification with God Who loves you. He invests Himself wholly into you. You become Him. "He that is joined to the Lord is one spirit."

As you grasp this concept, you will become more and more aware of the error that pervades false religion. You'll hear and react to even well intended words of duality, distance, demand, delay and denial. There is no abundant life in false religion. Walk away from those who teach duality.

You are one with Him.

TRUTH:

False religion separates, subjugates and denigrates. Faith (and the best of churches) confer unity, empowerment and value.

PRAYER:

Father, I've grown up in a culture with deep roots saturated in both the blessings and the curses of religion. You said that, as I come to know the Holy Spirit in me, that He will lead me into all truth. I ask You, God, to show me the treasures and precious truths, as well as the poisonous errors and untruths which I have unwittingly embraced. Reveal them to me, Father, and give me the courage to humbly embrace the good, even as I discard and step beyond any teaching which is not in agreement with Yourself. You are a God of Truth. I am one with You. Bless me, Father. Lead me, Father. Be the Good Shepherd in my life. Lead me home.

EXERCISE:

I believe that the anointing, the favor of God sets people free. It removes burdens and breaks yokes. As you leave your church service, ask yourself whether your Sunday morning is a freedom experience, a lifting of burdens, a breaking of yokes. (Isaiah 10:27) Is it a celebration of what God has done in and for you, or it a lesson that you really need to do this or this or this to satisfy an unhappy and scrupulous God, to make Him smile, or to earn His blessing, provision or reward? Is the message you hear there about one-ness or duality? Is it about peace on Earth and good will toward men, or is it about judgment, accusation and demand? Pray for discernment, and ask God to speak to you about your response to His revelation.

What Does a Walk with God Look Like?

Chapter 22

The Ultimate Arrogance

"In this is love, not that we loved God, but that He loved us and sent His Son to be the propitiation for our sins." **1 John 4:10**

It seems like the ultimate form of arrogance.

Linda came into my life through hospice. A tall woman with broad shoulders, Linda has known seasons of deep poverty. She walks with a slight stoop that I think was inflicted upon her simply by periods of lack, abuse, and being absolutely taken for granted. She was homeless once for three years, sleeping on the floor of an abandoned house. Even as I've known her, she weathered the last days of many, many months in serious hunger because she had either mis-spent some vital portion of her monthly income or, just as often, gave it away to someone else in need.

Linda served as caregiver for her invalid mom for long years and astounded the hospice staff with the quality of her service in that role. She loved her mom deeply. At the same time, make no mistake, her mom was a handful. Her mama loved to sing LOUDLY! Despite her Alzheimers, she could pick up the words to some Hank Williams honky-tonk ditty and fit it seamlessly into the tune of "Victory in Jesus" and then reverse herself, singing the words to "Victory in Jesus" to the tune of the same ribald honky-tonk standard.

The first time I met Linda, God transformed her life. As Linda prayed with me to receive God's life and forgiveness, He healed her completely of end-stage congestive heart failure, a diagnosis which included a prognosis of death in two to six months. What amazed me even more was how easily Linda grasped deep spiritual truths, even understanding how those related to other truths yet unspoken. Linda was and is an absolute thrill to teach.

Within months of her salvation, Linda was hearing God's voice, carrying on conversations with Him, and easily pouring that into the lives of others. One day, she was almost physically vibrating with joy. "David!" she told me, "God told me this morning that I am His favorite! David! I am His favorite!" Over the next several days, she told dozens of people that, and, while no one knew exactly how to respond, her joy was so infectious that no one argued with her.

Then one day, she called me. "David, God corrected me this morning," she said. "He told me, 'Linda, I didn't say you are my 'favorite.' I said 'favored,' not 'favorite.' Linda, I can't have favorites.' I feel kind of foolish, David, but, it's okay. He said it's okay. Somewhere deep inside I still know that He's just saying that. I really am His favorite."

It seems arrogant, but it's not. It seems braggadocios and boastful, but it's not. It seems prideful (and it can be), but the truth which lies here has nothing to do with pride. This truth may be the most overlooked, most denied and most completely ignored truth in all of the Scripture. But it's true. It's fundamental. And it's vitally necessary to understand.

Here it is: our walk with God begins when we grasp from the heart that it's not about us pursuing God but is all about the fact that He pursues us. Each of us is, in fact, His favorite.

Linda is in truth beautiful because God says she's beautiful. She is worthy because God has declared her worthy. She is gifted because God chose to give gifts to her. She is redeemed because Christ valued her enough to endure the torture of crucifixion in order to gain her companionship. She is well because He payed for her wellbeing. She is highly favored. She is awesome, wonderful, gifted, beautiful, sanctified, liberated, strong, graceful, as righteous as Christ Himself, crowned with glory and majesty, an heir to the wealth of the Kingdom of God, a ruler right here on the Earth. All because He says so.

As much as anyone, Linda is truly His favorite.

There's nothing quite as uncomfortable as trying to deal with a cowering dog. You know the kind–body contorted and shivering, tail between his legs with the very end twitching in miserable supplication, approaching you sideways so as to be ready to run at the slightest hint of opposition, and yet STARVING for any scrap of favor, any indication of simple acceptance.

A dog like that is painful to watch and impossible to relate to, and yet that's where many "Christians" live. Pathetic, self-consciously, painfully plaintive, begging but not receiving, cloaked in self-condemnation, without faith or joy or understanding or freedom or grace or any of the treasures that He has lavished upon them and yearns to see them grasp. They cling tenaciously to their right to camp out in the foyer and will fight not only to remain there but to deny their ownership or any suggested right to enjoy the rest of the house.

Linda knows God's favor, and it has transformed her character. She owns the whole estate, and she knows it. She celebrates her wealth and pours it out on others. She is royalty, even in hard circumstances.

The very first step in walking with God is to quit cowering and posturing. Instead, trust in His acceptance. The Christian life is not about our success or failure in pursuing Him; the Christian life is about the fact that He pursues us. Our calling is simply to receive. As we receive more and more freely, we overflow so that, through us, He can successfully pursue people all around us.

Another analogy.

My wife, Debbie, snores. It used to bother me. I'd wake up to this troubling noise and be unable to drift back into sleep. Then I'd transfer my aggravation to her by waking her up, asking her to turn over, accusing her of robbing me of sleep.

One night, God changed all that. "Dave," God whispered, "each breath Debbie takes is like music to me. Each breath is a testimony to the life that's in her. Each breath is a reminder of the joy of your youth, the body and soul which bore you two sons, a life laid down day after day for your wellbeing and fulfillment. Each breath is precious, Dave! Celebrate her snoring! It's cause for praise and worship!"

Everything changed. When Debbie snores, I praise God! I get drunk on His favor. I rejoice over the amazing riches He has lavished upon me in the body and breath of my wife! I lie there completely still, full of wonder at His goodness. I love Him and love her until my mind reels with the breathless realization of my wealth! And then, somewhere along the way, I fall back asleep and sleep like I never slept before.

But sometimes I'll say, "Deb, you were really tired last night."

"Why?" she says, like I'm accusing her. "Was I snoring?"

"All night," I might say. Or, "Yes. Some." Or, "A little. You were sleeping really soundly."

Right away, she's mortified! Horror stricken! Anguished! "Oh," she says, "I'm so sorry! I apologize! I feel so bad! I guess I'll have to sleep in the living room! I should sleep in the Lazy Boy. Why didn't you wake me up? Gosh, I feel terrible! I'm so sorry!"

A hundred times now, I've tried to explain to her, but, somehow, she hasn't received it. She doesn't get it. She hears me, but she doesn't believe. And the result is that (1) she is so worried about her snoring that she doesn't sleep well at all for several nights, getting up and moving to the other room at the slightest suspicion that she may be waking me up, and, (2) out of her concern, I am robbed of the joy of God's reminding me of her goodness and the consummate joy she is in my life.

So what about you?

Are you God's favorite? Do you understand that your snoring doesn't bother Him? Can you cast off the accusing voice of the enemy, quit cowering and posturing, and simply relax in His joyful acceptance? Can you receive the measure of His regard for you? Can you walk with Him, at ease in His Presence and confident of His favor? Can you see yourself as awesome? Beautiful? Righteous? Sanctified? Worthy? Redeemed and made spotless? A suitable companion for the Lord of the Universe?

"Come now, my love," He says. "Let's take a walk."

TRUTH:

No one wants to spend time with a companion who is convinced of his unworthiness, mired in self-loathing, and constantly apologizing for actual or assumed shortcomings. Give God a break. Pray that God reveal the wonder of your being, the glory of your friends and co-workers, and rejoice in the person He made you to be.

PRAYER:

Lord, thank You that You have declared me worthy of Your love. Thank You that You love even my snoring, that You have accounted for and paid for my stumblings, that You can make and have redeemed my deepest faults and failures. Thank You that You not only love me but have declared me worthy of that love. Thank You that, regardless of what we call facts, what You declare is truth. Thank You that truth will always trump facts. Thank You that I am spotless and beautiful. Thank You that there is peace between us. Thank you that I'm awesome–and that saying that is okay. Thank you. Thank you. Thank you.

EXERCISE:

Many times as I have encountered demoniacs, dark spirits which possess their bodies and minds will actually physically choke their victim rather than allow him or her to declare the favor of God. Demons can't bear the sound of the truth. They can't stay in a body where, in the power and authority of the Holy Spirit, the possessed person suddenly begins to proclaim life and grace and favor. The truth sets us free, and the SOUND of that truth sets us free. Take time now to stand in front of a mirror, lock eyes with your reflection, and declare the truth of God's favor emphatically to yourself. If need be, read this chapter aloud into the air of your bedroom. Declare your identity in your kitchen. Sanctify your car by the proclamation of God's favor in your life. Speak it out. Speak. Speak and believe.

Chapter 23

Christic in You

"Christ in you, the hope of glory." Col. 1:27

It was Sunday morning, and I didn't check my messages until almost noon. When I did, four urgent pleas from one of my closest spiritual sisters cried out to me. With her beautiful copper complexion, Anne and I come from totally different backgrounds. God saved Anne out of poverty, crack addiction and a sad life on mean streets; the measure of her change left her with a new and deeper addiction, an unquenchable appetite for the Word of God and Bible study. She studies 24/7.

This morning Anne was panicked. Her own mother had died of a nightmarish case of cancer, a curse that carved out a gaping softball-sized hole in her chest. Now, this morning, Anne was told that her daughter-in-law, Lelanna, had a lump the diameter of a quarter behind her left nipple. As if that by itself wasn't bad enough, Anne had also discovered that Lelanna was being waked up every night by a palpable spirit of fear in the room where she and her husband Levi slept. Both the prospect of breast cancer and the presence of some ungodly spirit in Anne's home were entirely unacceptable.

When I drove up in front of Anne's little house, Lelanna proved gracious and open. Four of us—me, Anne, Lelanna and Levi—settled into Anne's tiny living room. The young couple prayed together to receive Christ, and Lelanna freely shared about an excruciating childhood of emotional and physical abuse.

Then we climbed a dark and narrow staircase to the little get-away Levi and Lelanna had framed up in what had been the attic of Anne's old house. Since they had both just prayed so fervently for the Holy Spirit to come and take up residence inside of their bodies, I wasn't too concerned about any form of demonic oppression or possession. To be on the safe side, however, I asked LeLanna to lock eyes with me and allow me to speak past her own consciousness to any dark spirit that might still seek to control her mind and body. She readily consented. I began to call out and command any spirit opposed to the purposes of Christ in Lelanna. Not 15 seconds into that exercise, her whole body lurched violently with a deep abdominal spasm. Her breathed whooshed through her teeth in a sound that could have been a groan and a roar. She fell to all fours, for several minutes heaving and vomiting into a pan. When she rose up, washed and caught her breath, Lelanna was secure, separated, safe and resting now entirely within the Presence of God and God alone.

For some minutes, we then prayed over the room, ordering any spirit opposed to the lordship of Christ to leave and leave forever. That done, I felt Christ in me prompt us to re-address the painful lump that still sat in Lelanna's breast. This time, I placed Anne in the lead, instructing her as to how to effectively minister healing.

"Anne," I told her. "The Scripture says Christ Himself lives in you. To visualize that, I want you to see your body as a tent, like a little closet or pantry. You're in there. Christ is in there too–His mind, His will, His emotions, His Spirit. As you put your hands on Lelanna, I want you to picture both of you–Jesus and Anne–in that little tent, standing side by side. Now, you back up. Back right up against your backbone, and you push Jesus forward. Press Him. Now our hands are His hands, your voice is His voice, your authority is His authority, your command is His command. Christ is alive in you, Anne. Let Him heal Lelanna."

Anne grasped my teaching and, after a moment of eyes-closed communion with Christ, opened her eyes with a new expression. There was confidence there, stalwart assurance, even a taste of anger and surprise that this thing would invade, trespass upon a treasure as rich as the body of her daughter-in-law. Anne began to speak to the lump, the swelling, the soreness and discomfort in Lelanna's breast like it was a dog, stumbling into her kitchen and needing to be thrown out. When she stopped, I had Lelanna turn her back, reach inside her bra, and re-examine her own condition. Four more times, Anne and I cursed that dog, and, at the close of the fifth short session, the entire lump–along with all pain, soreness, inflammation and swelling–had disappeared entirely.

Now stop and consider the deeper truths behind this true story.

Seven years ago now, the idea that Lelanna could be healed in such a fashion was completely foreign to me. Then my niece, a non-believer, developed abdominal cancer.

I set about the best way I knew how to secure healing for my niece. I prayed diligently for her. I studied the Scripture and was assured by Christ's words, over and over again, that whatever I asked in His name would be granted to me. "Ask and it shall be given to you," Jesus taught, continuing, "What man is there of you, whom if his son ask bread, will he give him a stone? Or if he ask a fish, will he give him a serpent? If ye then, being evil, know how to give good gifts unto your children, how much more shall your Father which is in heaven give good things to them that ask him?" (Matt. 7:7-11) Over a dozen times, Jesus promises that God will hear and answer our prayers; I catalogued all of them. I saw God as more eager to answer respond to my needs than I was to ask.

Yet Michelle died.

So a conflict erupted in my life. Either I was incorrectly interpreting Scripture, or God's word was not reliable. I had to know which was true. I had to step past religious traditions. I had to move past erroneous teachings, limitations of my own experience, arguments of naysayers. I went directly to God, sought His face, wrestled with Scripture, and explored the implications of His day-by-day revelation. I began to experience the reality of His Presence inside me. I discovered our one-ness.

Now, I know that He lives inside me. The Creator of the Universe. The Risen Christ. The Lord of Lords. The Rock of Ages. The God of Abraham, Isaac and Jacob. He who healed the sick and then rose up from the dead. He lives inside me, and He, from inside me, will heal.

Slowly new dimensions of His presence unfolded in my consciousness, and a fresh confidence emerged. When my first healing happened,

I told a beautiful young woman who had lost much of her peripheral vision that I was going to let Christ in me speak to her eyes and that her eyes would then be healed. I did, and her eyes were healed instantly. She was ecstatic, weeping, saying over and over again, "Mr. Dave! I'm healed! He healed me!" Looking straight ahead, she marveled that she could identify someone standing in the doorway beside and almost behind her, that she could follow her own hands until they were spread on the same plane as her shoulders. Ten minutes later when she told her husband that God had healed her eyes, his first response was to say, "No, baby, no. He didn't. God doesn't heal people like that any more." And the healing she had just experienced evaporated like steam from a kettle.

It was enough for me. It was a start.

Now, Christ in me doesn't tell me to pray over everybody. But when He nudges me to act, I act with confidence, and healing unfolds more often than not. When healing doesn't happen, reasons manifest; when those reasons are addressed, more healings happen. I have power over demons. I know that, when I walk into a room, spiritual powers take notice. Christ lives in me. I don't talk too much about walking in power and victory, believe it or not, but, because I know His presence, increasing authority and more frequent victories have become reality in my life.

Christ Himself calls us–Every believer! All of us!–to walk in the power of His indwelling Presence. He lives inside us for a purpose, to express His compassion and demonstrate His love to everyone around us. Through us, He wants to touch people who hurt, who suffer, who need, who weep, who struggle, who dream and yearn but have not yet grasped, or who simply survive in day-to-day darkness and bewilderment.

It is God's heart to love all of us deeply; it is also His heart to use our hands as believers, our voices, our eyes, our hearts to demonstrate His character, His truth, His promises, His Presence to others.

Christ lives in you. Christ lives in you. You are one with Him.

What does that mean in your day-to-day existence?

TRUTH:

Christ lives in you. A God of deep compassion, His intent is to love you boundlessly and, through you, to reach others. If you let Him, He will do that through your heart, your voice, your hands.

PRAYER:

Father, thank You that, by the far limits of your grace, You have deemed me worthy of Your love, that You have invested Your own Being, Your own Spirit, Your own Self into my body. Thank you, Father, that I have this privilege, to be Your vessel, Your home, Your child–to be one with You. Thank you. As you live inside of me, Lord, let me come to know Your Presence ever more deeply. Be real to me. Break out of every confining belief in my life. Tear down every wall between us. Be so rich, so radiant in my being that others will be drawn to You through Your power in my hands, Your voice on my lips, Your radiance in my countenance. Use me, God, to draw others into this amazing one-ness with You.

EXERCISE:

Put a sign on your bathroom mirror that says simply "Christ lives in me. I am the hope of glory. Col. 1:27" or "He that is joined to the Lord is one spirit. 1 Cor. 6:17." Read it out loud every morning and every night, and let your mind become more and more aware of your unity with Him.

Chapter 24

You in Christ

"What is man, that thou art mindful of him?" **Psalm 8:4**

It was Sunday morning. As He often does, God spoke to me in the shower, this time handing me a riddle to be answered later that day. " Today, Dave," He said, "I'll teach you to love from the inside out."

"God," I replied, "I think I know that already. You know the lesson You gave me about the little closet, the tabernacle where You live here inside of me? I've got that, Lord. I just reach here into my innermost being where I am one in Spirit with You. You, in turn, pour out Your love from inside me into the lives of other people. Isn't that 'loving people from the inside out'?"

"Yes, but that's not what I'm talking about," He said and repeated, "Today I'll teach you to love people from the inside out."

Three hours later, I walked into our mid-day church service and noticed right away something was very different. My church, which normally does a great job reaching out to a non-traditional demographic, had become a bikers' convention. All around me, there were black leather, chains, spikes and studs, scars, tattoos on top of wrinkles, combat boots, grizzled cheeks and road-worn faces. A Hollywood director could have found all of the extras here, male and female, for a good pirate movie. It was Uglies Unlimited. I wasn't intimidated, but I took note and wondered what was up.

Pastor Quinton stepped up to the microphone, launched into an opening welcome and prayer. Then he kicked off our worship time. singing "Teach Me to Love You from the Inside Out." It wasn't exactly what God had nudged me about in the shower, but it was close enough to tip me off that the lesson He had promised in the shower hand commenced.

God's voice resonated through my mind and heart again. "Dave, you're correct in that you've learned to draw power out of our one-ness, and, in that sense, together, you and I 'love people from the inside out.' But that's not the exercise this morning. That practice which you know, that's all about Me in you, my indwelling Spirit. That's Me in you. What I want to show you now is you in Me. I want to show you what it looks like to understand not "Me in you" but "you in Me." I want you to see through the filter of My Presence. I want you to understand that you are inside of Me and work through Me in everything you do."

"Bow your head and close your eyes," He told me. I did, and the lesson continued.

"Dave," He said, "you've begun to learn the measure of My love for you, and that's good. But the truth is that I love ALL men like that. I love EVERYONE. From the very day when I fashioned Adam's frame out of the muck and mire of Earth, I've delighted in the sons of men– their potential for greatness, their passion and energy, their curiosity and creativity, their ability to love, to bless, to share, to house and share My Spirit. Saved or lost, I love them all. I love their physical bodies, Dave. I made them–opposable thumbs, smiles and eyes, hair color and symmetry, all the curves and angles. They get pretty wrinkled, crooked and battle-weary, Dave, but they're beautiful to Me. This morning, I'm going to let you see them through My eyes."

"Whoa!" I breathed silently.

"Now raise up your head and look around," He told me.

I slowly lifted my head, opened my eyes, and was stunned. The bikers who had crowded into the church, festooned in worn leather and chains, were transformed into the most breath-takingly beautiful people I had ever beheld. They sparkled. They glowed as if they had showered in liquid grace. They glistened with the golden love of Christ. Each one was more exquisite, more marvelous, more handsome than the one before. I was blown away, fascinated, tearing my vision away from one man only to be captivated by the dazzling countenance of a woman in the very next row. I literally cried, my heart leaping and pounding, pushing at the confines of my chest, full to bursting. I stood there weeping, consumed by wonder, joy, pride in the handiwork of God, and gratitude for this incredibly privileged perspective.

That wonder has never left me. Now, among Indian beggars or Hospice patients, looking at oozing craters carved into their bodies by the nightmare of cancer or seeing them buried alive in the labyrinth of Alzheimers, among hardened criminals or people so lost in loneliness or neglect that they slash and dig pits in their own arms and legs, I can put on the lenses of His Presence and see them through Him. I look through His eyes, through this unimaginable quality of love that sanctifies the most unholy, the most rank, the most despicable, the most profane and wasted of men. He LOVES us! He loves ALL of us!

"For God so loved the world..." reads John 3:16. Not "For God so loved Christians." Not "For God so loves good boys and girls." Not "church-goers." Not "tithers." Not just the compassionate, the beautiful, the popular, the rich, the morally upstanding, or the mentally or physically sound. Not just heterosexuals, white people, Americans, cowboys, Presbyterians, Roman Catholics, kids, old people, or those free of criminal records or intent. He loves all of us!

Look! Look! Look at this: "And He, that same Jesus Himself, is the propitiation, the atoning sacrifice for our sins, and not for ours alone but also for the sins of the <u>whole world</u>." (1 John 2:2) Or this: "For therefore we both labour and suffer reproach, because we trust in the living God, <u>who is the Saviour of all men, specially of those that believe</u>." (1 Tim. 4:10) And then there's this: "But God commendeth his love toward us, in that, <u>while we were yet sinners</u>, Christ died for us." (Romans 5:8)

Do you realize that every soul that ends up in Hell goes there with his or her sins entirely forgiven? He died for ALL of us! He carried ALL of our sin, ALL of the darkness in our lives, ALL of our failings and heartless motivations in His body to the cross. There, gasping for every excruciating breath, fastened to rough-hewn planks, filled perhaps even to His capacity with every imaginable form of evil (all of which He was entirely innocent), He locked your sin and my sin into a literal death-grip and carried it into the deepest entrails of death. When He rose up three days later, He rose up alone. He rose up clean, sanctified, absolutely holy. He rose on Easter Sunday victorious over all.

So this God comes, in one form or another, to each person ever born anywhere on this planet. He reaches out with this priceless package, the gift of His own righteousness, cradled in His palms. "Here," He says. "I bought this for you. It cost me my life, but it's free to you. Here." Your response to that invitation determines your eternal destination.

Now note this: I said, "So God comes, in one form or another..."

"One form or another" means me. "One form or another" means you. "One form or another" means each of us who, by faith, embrace that gift fully and learn to walk, like Noah, in one-ness with the One who gave Himself for us.

He uses us. He partners with us. It's NOT just His nail-scarred hands that hold forth this precious package; He holds forth your hands. My hands. Our hands. He lets us, on His behalf, offer His love and righteousness to those for whom His heart flames with longing. We get to love bikers, prostitutes, tax collectors, burdened moms, distracted dads, child molesters, gossips, the fearful and hateful and those who seek to destroy us...because He loves them first. We have this privilege. We act as partners, ambassadors, one spirit, one mind, one intent with Him. We are one with Him.

In us and through us, the Scripture says, God has chosen to make His love complete. We get to make His love perfect, to see His love fulfilled.

"His love is perfected in us"! (1 John 4:12)

How good is God?

How rich is that?

TRUTH:

God loves you in your very darkest places. If you'll let Him, He will use you to love others the same way.

PRAYER:

Father, I may not have ever grasped before this moment the depth of Your love for me. Thank you, Father. Thank You. Thank You that You made me beautiful. Thank You that I can look like You, In the gift of Your one-ness with me, teach me to love others with that same transforming power and intensity. Thank you, again! You are an amazing God!

EXERCISE:

Take a ride on a city bus or a long walk through a public place. Watch the people there. Ask God in you to give you an appreciation for their humanity, for His handiwork, for His delight in them. (Prov. 8:31) Ask Him for His vision, His perspective as you observe passers-by. Listen for His voice and respond to the prompting of His Spirit.

Chapter 25

Giving: The Privilege of Sonship

"When they came to Capernaum, those who collected the two-drachma tax came to Peter and said, 'Does your teacher not pay the two-drachma tax?' He said, 'Yes.' And when he came into the house, Jesus spoke to him first, saying, 'What do you think, Simon? From whom do the kings of the earth collect customs or poll-tax, from their sons or from strangers?' When Peter said, 'From strangers,' Jesus said to him, 'Then the sons are exempt.'"
Matt. 17:24-26

I give. I don't limit myself to a tithe.

There's a huge difference between giving and tithing, and the truth runs completely contrary to common teaching.

Tithing is a function of the Law.

Any argument against that statement fails.

The tithe is founded upon a perception that God's favor is conditional, that His blessing, His provision depends upon you giving first. If you tithe, He will bless you. If you don't tithe, then He will cause your money to fly away like chaff in the wind. That's what's preached, and that's the Law. **Conditional favor** is the essence of the Law. (Deut. 30) Jesus set us free from the Law. (Romans 7:1-6) As believers, we ALWAYS walk in His favor. His favor toward us is in no way conditional to what we do.

Whom did Jesus bless? Do you think the Samaritan woman in John 4 was a faithful tither? How likely was it that the woman taken in adultery in John 8 spent much time measuring out her weekly offering? What about Zacchaeus in Luke 19? What about when the Scripture says, "Great multitudes followed him, and he healed them all"? Do you think he had the apostles go among the multitude first to ask who was caught up on their tithe?

On the other hand, whom did Jesus castigate? The Pharisees, who tithed publicly and scrupulously. Jesus pronounced judgment upon them as sons of Satan, hypocrites and white-washed tombs. People who scrupulously tithed crucified Christ, and it was those who failed to tithe–sinners!–with whom Christ ate and upon whom He lavished blessings.

Now don't get excited and run off into license, choosing to slash your giving to nothing or walking away from your pledge to the building campaign! The end of this process is NOT to offer you an excuse to give less, but to unveil the freedom you have to give much, much more.

Like I said, I give. A lot.

In 1999, we took our first trip into eastern Romania. In less than two weeks there, God knit my heart to that of a young Romanian mission pastor named Florin Gheorghe. Since then, I've trekked back to Romania over and over again, always connecting with Florin and his family, delighting in laughter and tears, shared meals and ministry.

In 2007, Florin's sponsoring church weathered a painful split, and the financial support they provided dried up completely. A hard worker in a hugely depressed economy, Florin boarded a train and found a job in a glass foundry in Italy. One morning, he called me from there in tears. "David," he wept, "what am I doing here? I am a husband separated from my wife, a father separated from my sons, a pastor wrenched away from my church. This is so wrong. What am I doing here?"

A few weeks later at about 4:30 in the morning, I was kneeling in my living room, my head down in the seat of an cushioned chair, pressing through what seemed like a loooong season of dry and restless prayer. Suddenly, God spoke. "David," He said in a voice as undeniable as the sunrise, "I want you to take responsibility for Florin's financial support."

"Whoa, God! Whoa!" was my initial response! My mind sprinted over the very short extent of our finances. "NOW you want to talk?

Look, I don't have that kind of money! What are we talking–three or four hundred a month?"

"Five hundred," He responded. "Every month. Listen now; I didn't ask you if you had the money. I have the money. What I want you to do is to deliver it for Me. I have the money. You just be the delivery boy."

I was not convinced. I argued with Him for 20 minutes before capitulating under only one condition, that He explain this venture to Debbie.

What immediately followed was the most profound revelation of my life, an impartation so supernatural that I've shared details with very few people. For now, I'll only say the intensity of that experience so boggled my mind that I told God, "Lord, if don't have some sign that this actually happened, I'll wake up in two weeks and decide it was only a dream."

I was still blown away two hours later when I got to my office at the school. Walking in, I found an envelope on my desk, an envelope I had not left there the night before. On a roughly torn section of paper ripped from a legal pad, one of my school parents had scrawled a note. "Dear Mr. Diamond, God woke me up at 4:30 this morning and put your friends in Romania all over my mind. Please use this as you see fit." I unfolded the check that was tucked away, hidden in the envelope. It was $500.

We support Florin now and several others as well.

Take time now to understand this much larger truth. <u>Your Father owns the universe.</u> He made it. Forget the Bible verse about His owning cattle on a thousand hills; according to British astronomers, He causes the skies of Neptune and Jupiter to rain diamonds. The oil or gold we fight over because of its scarcity He sowed into the depths of the Earth like you and I would water a pot of geraniums. He not only owns ALL of the real estate on Earth; He owns the sunrise. He can whisper Kingdoms into being and raise up riches as easily as you and I daydream. His wealth stretches the meaning of "infinite." If He ever runs short of anything, He can murmur it into being.

That's your daddy. Your Father. Your husband. Your brother. Your bridegroom. Your love. That's "Jehovah-jireh"– God Who Provides.

And, get this: we don't even have to ask God for anything. Whatever we need, He has already given to us! Note the past tense: "has given"–as in already accomplished, finished, done, completed with such extravagant abandon that we never need raise the question again. Look at 1 Peter 1:3–"His divine power **hath given** unto us **ALL things** that pertain unto life and godliness, through the knowledge of Him that hath called us to glory and virtue." Or Ephesians 1:3–"Blessed be the God and Father of our Lord Jesus Christ, who **hath blessed** us with ALL spiritual blessings in heavenly places in Christ."

As a believer awakened by God to the voice of the Holy Spirit, I am directed by Him in a moment-by-moment conversation. I dance, following His lead, to divine music and direction rising up from deep within the inner currents of the Trinity. My resources, as His child, are absolutely endless. Under His direction, I can, by faith, give away EVERYTHING and know without a shadow of a doubt that He will replenish my supply to facilitate my giving even more.

The greatest evidence of the coming of the Holy Spirit on the day of Pentecost was not tongues of fire, not miraculous languages, not the sound of rushing wind, not even 3,000 souls being saved. The greatest evidence of the Holy Spirit was that believers "sold their possessions and goods, and parted them to all men, as every man had need." (Acts 2:45)

I urge you as strongly as I can, dearly beloved, let God set you free. If a God of infinite wealth and generosity lives inside of you, and if it is indeed His deepest nature to give and give and give more, how can you as His child fret and labor and hesitate, limiting His generosity to your wee ten percent? Believe. Listen, and give "according to His riches"!

Trust Him.

Just give.

TRUTH:

As a child of God, you hold God's promise to provide EVERY-THING you need to fulfill the calling He holds for your life. In the light of that purpose, your financial resources are limitless.

PRAYER:

Father, I thank You that You have promised to meet all of my need, that You have ALREADY given me ALL things pertaining to life and Godliness! Teach me to hear Your voice. Teach me to be bold in giving, to hear Your voice and recognize those circumstances in which I can lavish financial support on people and ministries. Teach me not only to walk every day in that extravagant quality of Your love but to share that extravagance freely with others. Save me from selfishness and fear, Lord. Teach me to give.

EXERCISE:

As I shared before in my story about my dad, I lived for a long time with a lot of fear and mistrust in regard to money. I know what it's like to feel God's prompting to share meager resources and have that accompanied by a tightening of my chest and a rising gorge of anxiety in the pit of my stomach. As I grew to recognize that such fear was not of God (2 Tim. 1:7) but was of the enemy, I consciously determined to slap the enemy in the face on every such occasion and would give MORE rather than less to the person or ministry at hand.

His faithfulness proved so true and His provision so consistent that I began to apply the same principle to my over-all ministry finances as well. When money seemed most precarious and fear manifested, I began to pray, "God! Show me to whom I should give!" Then, listening to His promptings again, I would cut a check and bless whomever He indicated.

Chapter 26

The Holy Spirit Speaks

"Now the Spirit speaketh expressly" **1 Tim. 4:1**

The first time my best friend, Jeremy Mangerchine, and I went to Kolkota, we stayed in a Catholic retreat center about a block from Mother Teresa's home. It was low rent, believe me. On the minus side, the walls were mildewed and the floor gritty, blonde roaches came out at night, and the water supply was pretty temperamental. But, on the plus side, our room featured a gargantuan antique air conditioner that roared at night like a hurricane, and the kitchen served huge amounts of food and some of the best chai in the world.

Every morning there, I learned to check first thing for a text from my beautiful wife, Debbie, who was still in Louisiana, eleven time zones removed, but who prayed for us continuously. In the wee wee hours, I would usually receive a lengthy text from her. Most included cautions, counsel and concerns which the Lord had shared with her in Louisiana, using her prophetic gift and AT&T's unlimited texting as His means of communicating with us on the other side of the globe in India.

One morning in particular, we were scheduled to begin the first of two three-day seminars on healing and deliverance. We had made plans for an audience of 135 to 185 people. We had arranged for appropriate hall space and meal service, and were hopeful that our estimations might prove to be conservative. On previous ventures, we had delivered the same seminars to crowds of at least 200 to more than 500 participants. But that morning, Debbie wrote to us from Louisiana, "God's word for you today is this: do not be disappointed today. The attendees to your conference will be very small in number. Do not be disappointed or discouraged. This is God's doing and is according to His plan."

Thirty-five people showed up.

But, in that number sat a highly respected bishop and at least 20 pastors, a handful of workers with the Kolkota City Mission, an Irish missionary and a small collection of teenagers. The small size of the audience afforded us the opportunity to field questions and the intimacy to effectively minister even as we taught. It was a sweet, sweet time. Out of that experience, we saw churches transformed and received invitations to come and share our ministry in some of India's most important urban centers. We were not disappointed. We were elated.

The funny thing about this story is that Debbie never knew she could speak for the Holy Spirit through at least 25 years of our Christian life. It's not that she didn't hear Him. We were taught that women should be silent and, second, that the Holy Spirit never spoke to anyone directly ever after the Scripture was compiled. Finally, Debbie simply doubted herself. She was "modest" and "humble" enough that, even when she was prompted by the Holy Spirit to speak, she felt unworthy, awkward, and almost always held her tongue.

Finally one day, as she attended a church service, someone spoke a word from God to Debbie. "Mrs. Diamond," this previously unknown minister said, "you have a prophetic gift, and you need to let God develop that for you. There are many, many times when you'll see a person or be praying for someone, and you'll hear a voice tell you something about what that person is feeling or thinking or, perhaps, something they need to know. God wants to use you to be His mouthpiece, to encourage and build up people. Instead, when you hear His voice, you're thinking, 'No, they won't listen to me. This is kind of crazy. I can't possibly say that.' God's word to you is to speak, to pass on the things He whispers to you as He directs, and, in the process, both you and they will be blessed."

Let's just say this: Mrs. Diamond is silent no more.

And I am extremely grateful for it.

Understand this: the Holy Spirit speaks to every born-again believer. To believe otherwise is patently foolish. Just ask yourself, "How can the God of the universe, the God Who spoke all of Heaven and Earth into being, live inside me for year after year and remain silent? How can the Spirit whom Jesus promised would "lead us into all truth" do that without ever uttering a word? How can we say that we have a relationship with God if we can't ever hear His voice?

The truth is that the Holy Spirit really likes to talk. That doesn't mean that He talks all the time. Sometimes He's quiet for a season, but then there are these other times when you want to say, "Wait! What? Can you back up again and repeat that? You're going too fast! I can't keep up!" As we've said, He is intensely relational, and relationship is all about these three things: (1) communication, (2) communication, and (3) communication.

So how do you hear the Holy Spirit?

You listen.

Sometimes I talk to Him first, speaking out thanks for all that He is in my life or asking Him what's on His mind for the day. Other times, I just like to sit and not say anything until I feel His Presence, allowing my silence to be the unspoken invitation. Other times, especially when I have trouble reining in my thoughts and imagination, I simply ask Him to wash me, speaking over and over again until His Presence washes over me in waves. I know then that we're communicating even if we never step beyond absolute silence. More often, as I slip into that place of rest, His voice is suddenly there, soft, quiet, gentle, transforming.

Very often, I read Scripture first to settle my mind and heart and enter into a place where I am more focused on the things of God and less distracted by my surroundings or the pressures of life. Debbie also likes the *Jesus Calling* series and *Streams in the Desert*. I like devotionals by Smith Wigglesworth or Watchman Nee or the sermons of John G. Lake.

My best friend Jeremy likes to speak in the Spirit until He feels the same captivating Presence. Then he too often lapses into silence, carrying on long conversations with God simply in His mind, Jeremy framing questions and God responding. Sometimes He takes Jeremy places or answers Jeremy's questions in pictures or short "film clips."

Why don't we hear the Holy Spirit more often?

I'd like to offer two possible answers.

First, Jeremy one time asked God Himself that question, and God gave Him an unforgettable vision. It was early, early morning and Jeremy and the Holy Spirit were having a quiet party together. "Why," Jeremy asked, "don't we do this all of the time? Why do I go through so much of my day without clearly hearing this conversation?"

Immediately before him appeared a rectangle like a large-screen TV with the face of God in the middle as if He was one of TV's talking heads. Looking directly into Jeremy's eyes, God began saying, "I'm talking. I'm talking. I'm talking. I'm talking." Then, in space around God, things began to appear–traffic, children playing, a New Orleans streetcar, people speaking at a lunch table, a street repair team, a motorcycle, a man cutting grass, etc.–each with its own accompanying noise.

God kept saying, "I'm talking. I'm talking. I'm talking." But, as the clutter behind Him piled up, God's voice was overwhelmed until Jeremy could not have known God was speaking at all except that His lips were still moving. When the box filled completely and His voice completely smothered, then, one by one, the elements of clutter began to dissolve until, once again, God was left alone, still saying, "I'm talking. I'm talking. I'm talking."

To hear God, you have to listen.

Secondly, many religious leaders teach that it is a very dangerous thing for the average believer to think that He can talk with God. That's worse than horse-hockey. That's deception. If you've been taught that practically all of your life, it may take some time at first to discern the Holy Spirit's voice. Just listen and be patient.

He's there. And He likes to talk.

TRUTH:

The Holy Spirit loves to speak. The question is only this: are you listening?

PRAYER:

Father, tune my ears and heart to the outpouring of the Holy Spirit. I recognize, Lord, that language is a gift, the foundation and facility of any relationship. I need to hear Your voice. I want to hear Your voice. Teach me. Sing to me. Instruct me. Correct me. Share your heart and mind with me. Lead me into understanding and constant awareness of the oneness that is ours. Speak to me, Lord. Teach me to listen and to hear. Speak to me.

EXERCISE:

Find a quiet place.

Sit and listen.

Chapter 27

The Love of God Perfected

"No one has seen God at any time; if we love one another, God abides in us, and His love is perfected in us." **1 John 4:12**

Why would God talk to us? Can't we just let the pastor hear from God and, then, we can show up on Sunday and the pastor can share God's word with us? Isn't that what we pay the pastor for? Can't we just read the Bible? Isn't that God's word? Isn't that enough?

Let's consider a recent interaction.

Just yesterday, I was driving home from Alabama. Passing the headquarters to a major corporation just off I-59, God prompted me, "Go check on Emma!" Realizing that this life-long friend was probably getting off of work, I swerved into the turn lane, drove into the parking lot, parked and took the elevator to her office.

Now understand this. I went to grammar school with Emma. I thought I knew her whole life. So, walking into her beautiful office, I was both warmly received and could see she was exhausted and struggling somehow. Was she free for a quick dinner? Yes. At the quiet restaurant, her weariness became clear. She was feeling threatened in her marriage, empty in her prayers, spiritually harassed, struggling to sleep, and frustrated and fruitless in her day-to-day existence. Always juggling an extremely active schedule, this mature Christian woman had fallen under the influence of accusation, shame and exhaustion.

Knowing that a prayer time might be emotional, I asked her if we could go and pray together in a local church. Once there, I asked permission to place my hand on her forehead, a practice by which God often downloads information and directs my ministry.

This time, I was in for a surprise. Here, lightly touching the forehead of a woman I had known and loved for decades, I suddenly heard the words "molested," "abused" and "violence." "Lord," I asked silently, "I've known this woman all of her life! When was she molested? Are You sure I'm hearing this correctly? I really don't want to go there."

"She was twelve," He responded. "Ask her."

So I did. "This is so strange, Emma," I said gently, "but were you a victim or a witness to some act of violence, some traumatic event perpetrated upon you or a family member when you were twelve years old?"

Her shocked expression and rush of tears confirmed the Spirit's direction. An older neighbor, a respected friend of the family molested Emma when she was twelve. Because of the man's reputation, her own parents didn't believe her story. And because the man was a neighbor, she could not escape his presence. Long gone, long ago dealt with, images of that horror had come flooding back recently, and the accuser had replowed ground, sowing tares of guilt and condemnation, shame and confusion into the rich fields of Emma's courage and faith. Nightmares prevented her from sleeping. She was having trouble relating to her husband. She suddenly felt unworthy, confused, torn and distracted.

As God lifted the veil on an area of spiritual attack, now Emma allowed Christ in me to rebuke this spiritual enemy who had gained entrance into her consciousness, not possessing but oppressing her spirit. We declared aloud the inherited righteousness of Christ in Emma. By the authority of Christ in us, we severed and cast away the soul-tie which every person enters into with any sexual partner. Out loud, Emma renounced every ungodly spiritual influence, resubmitted her mind to the cleansing of the Holy Spirit, and declared the truth of her one-ness in the heart of Her Savior. Tears flowed. Freedom dawned again. Emma left our meeting very much at peace, very much relieved, refocused not only on her own innocence but on the value of her husband's love for her. Just this morning she called and reported that she slept like a baby last night, woke up refreshed and thankful, is free again and invigorated for another day's walk with God.

Now let me ask this. Consider, in that transaction, the guidance I received from the gentle presence of the Holy Spirit. He prompted me to check on Emma. He revealed the root of her malaise in very specific terms, giving me passwords into some of the most vulnerable corners of her soul. He directed the conversation. He set Emma free.

Such pro-active guidance only comes through moment-by-moment leadership of the Presence of Christ in you. This is walking with God. This is one-ness. These are the kinds of conversations and activities that the two of you can share. This should be a the normal Christian life.

Here's an eye-popping, mind-bending, life-transforming truth. In John 14, Jesus is sharing one of His final interactions with His apostles. As He talks to them about His Father in Heaven. the Apostle Philip says, "Lord, show us the Father!"

Jesus responds, "Have I been so long with you, and yet you have not come to know Me, Philip? He who has seen Me has seen the Father; how can you say, 'Show us the Father'?" (John 14:8-9)

Do you understand that it is the desire and intent of your Creator that, when people look at YOU, they too will see the Father? Do you understand that when Paul talks about the "church" being the "body of Christ," he is NOT using an analogy? Do you understand that we actually ARE the body of Christ on this Earth, that, in the same way I tell my fingers to type out this sentence, God can tell each of us to go here, speak this, comfort this person, touch this child, support this ministry, pray for this woman, call this man, or stop in and check on Emma?

We are His body. That is not an analogy. We are His physical body. And, in that sense, as we touch and talk and counsel and give and pray and share and bless, we too can stand before men and hear God whisper, "He who has seen (**YOUR NAME HERE**) has indeed seen the Father."

Whoa! Whoa! Whoa!

Does that sound like another example of "the ultimate arrogance"?

It's not! It's what God intended us to be!

Why else would He endure the horrors of the cross? To surround Himself with namby-pamby do-gooders? To eternally wet-nurse a bunch of spiritual babies? To listen to us apologize for our failings and, denying our birthright, eternally reconfirm our mistaken identity as "sinners"? To hold us accountable to the Ten Commandments and then stand as judge of every detail of our mostly long and boring lives? To lease us a room in the foyer?

I don't think so.

Look again at 1 John 4:12: *"No one has seen God at any time; if we love one another, God abides in us, and His love is perfected in us."* Do you see why John starts off this verse by saying, "No man has seen God at any time"? Can you see that as "His love is perfected in us," people will look at you and see Christ? This is God's plan. This is God's invitation for your life–to allow Him to reveal Himself through you!

Look again at the opening verse. As we walk in one-ness, as we moment with Christ, we are His hands, His feet, His voice, His lips. Our presence reverberates to the pulse of His heartbeat. Our minds swirl with the rich goodness of His thoughts. Our hands and voices serve as channels of His majesty. His river of life springs up in us and, filling our consciousness, overflows into the lives of others around us.

That's what the Scripture means when John says, "His love is perfected in us"! The Amplified Bible says, His love "is brought to completion (to its full maturity, runs its full course, is perfected) in us!"

This is the essence of our calling–to be so joined and identified, to be so one with Christ that we actually are His Presence as we stand in the marketplace, the classroom, the office, the gymnasium, the parking lot or even church. In the gift of our one-ess, we get to be Him.

The love of God is perfected, completed, brought to fruition–in us!

Can you receive that?

TRUTH:

As we listen to and obey the Holy Spirit, we function as His body. His love for others is then made complete through us.

PRAYER:

Father, I love you! I don't want to be satisfied with less than all that You have for me. I want Your love to pour through me, Your wisdom to pour through me, Your healing power to pour through me, Your acceptance, Your grace, Your generosity, Your deepest knowledge of the deepest currents of men's minds and souls to pour through me. Teach me, Father, to hear and respond to Your voice. Knock down every obstacle. Silence every counterfeit. Tear down every erroneous teaching in my life. Let me know Your mind and heart in such depth that Your voice echoes in every word I speak. Possess me. Be my God. Be my Guide. Be my Father. I love you.

EXERCISE:

Ask God to give you a supernatural word of encouragement and blessing for someone in your next 24 hours. As you walk through this day then, be especially attuned to His Spirit. Listen. When He prompts you, don't hesitate. Obey. Back up in that little tabernacle against the very sinew and bone of your spinal column, and gently push Him forward. Give Him your mind, your voice, your feet and your hands. Then watch what happens.

Chapter 28

What He Won't Say and Will Say

"There is therefore now no condemnation to them which are in Christ Jesus, who walk not after the flesh, but after the Spirit." **Romans 8:1**

Praise God that there are some things that God can't do!

He can't lie. He can't renege on a promise. He can't contradict Himself. He can't get lost or confused, or fall into a bad mood and decide, like a mean kid with a spider, to pull off your legs just for fun.

He can't accuse believers either.

As I related earlier, I used to go to church years ago, eagerly anticipating that the pastor was going to "beat me up." It seemed like, every week, I would writhe around like an earthworm on hot concrete as the preacher would first make me feel like a disease, then tell me how much God loved me anyway, and finally encourage me to try to act like something other than a disease until I failed again and came back to church.

Man, what a miserable cycle that is!

As I grew in maturity, I wrapped the same concept in a little different language! "Thank God," I would say, "that the Holy Spirit 'convicted me' about that!" "That" could mean a five-minute foray into some form of pornography, a lie to a family member or colleague, an outburst of anger over some incompetent driver, etc., etc., etc.

It took me a long, long time to understand that the Holy Spirit does not "convict" believers. That means He does not "prove or declare someone guilty of an offense." He does not accuse, attack, charge, denounce, indict, prosecute, incriminate, libel or slander believers. He doesn't make believers feel guilty. He doesn't (in Southern Baptist lingo) "jump all over our toes."

The Scripture says that He convicts <u>the world</u> of sin. That's the unsaved, the unregenerate, those who have not yet received the gift of righteousness. He does not convict or accuse believers.

He can't.

His promise to us, recorded by God in Jeremiah 31:34, is this: "I will forgive their iniquity, and I will remember their sin no more." He can not accuse you of that which He does not remember.

In the New Testament, Satan stands as the accuser. Look at Rev. 12:10: "I heard a loud voice saying in heaven, Now is come salvation, and strength, and the kingdom of our God, and the power of his Christ: for the accuser of our brethren is cast down, which accused them before our God day and night."

What the Holy Spirit does is counsel, encourage and comfort you. He will correct but not condemn you. He will discipline but not demean you. He will teach you but never torment or threaten you. Like a good father, He will address behavior without ever attacking your identity. He will never speak or act in contradiction to the truth of the Scripture.

He will never speak in fear.

He will never be in a hurry.

He will very rarely force Himself upon you, insisting upon your attention at any given particular place or time.

He always honors faith.

He always loves. He always speaks the truth.

His voice transforms. His voice creates life.

Rodney is one of my best and most enduring friends. A former semi-pro football player, he's about as different from me as one can get and still fall into the same species. Where I tend to neglect my physical body, Rodney was at one time a beast on the football field and has always drawn confidence and strength out of his physical wellbeing.

So it came as a shock to Rodney when doctors diagnosed him with prostate cancer. True to form, he carefully examined the pros and cons of his medical options, and chose his course of action with as much wisdom and counsel and prayer as possible. Then radiation didn't eliminate the problem, and, after doctors removed his prostate entirely, his PSA count went up even more. Cancer still lurked somewhere in his body.

When definitive news came back, it wasn't good. "The cancer has moved into your pelvic bone, Rodney," said his physician. "There's nothing more we can do." It was a terminal diagnosis.

At that point, Rodney ventured into a pursuit of God's healing with greater gravity than I had seen before. He fought to understand and receive the wisdom of God. God spoke to Rodney in a number of ways.

First, he allowed Rodney to be present twice as a handful of us expelled demons from deeply suffering people. The first was a woman who, as the demon seized control, fell on the floor in Rodney's living room and tried to slither out the door. The second man cried out with fear and almost overwhelming chest pain as demonic forces left him and he was healed of stage-four cirrhosis.

Second, several prophetic voices surrounded Rodney, even to the person of his three-year-old granddaughter. That's right: three years old. The two of them, "Papa" Rodney and this precocious little girl, had curled up for an afternoon nap. After a few minutes of restful quiet, Zoe's little voice suddenly broke the afternoon stillness. "Papa?"

"Yes, Zoe."

"You know God is healing you."

"How do you know that, Zoe?" Rodney asked.

"I don't know, Papa. I just know it."

At his next doctors appointment, Rodney's PSA count had inexplicably dropped from over 6.0 to 0.08 and has continued to descend to entirely negligible levels.

Finally, Rodney came with me to visit a man who had been diagnosed with terminal cancer. Knowing the wisdom that had been imparted through Rodney's experience, I took a back seat in this interaction and learned from Rodney's testimony.

"Bill," Rodney told him, "to step into healing, you need to make a choice. As I explain that choice you can pick one position or the other, but you can't choose both. And you won't choose just once. You make the same choice a hundred times a day. You choose over and over again.

"Here it is. On the one hand, you have a thousand facts. The voices of your physicians, the evidence of pet-scans and biopsies and a hundred lab tests all render facts. Your PSA count is a fact. Your biopsy results are full of facts. Your doctors diagnosis is a fact. Your pain is a fact. Each pet-scan renders facts. Your loss of strength and energy is a fact. Your lost employment is a fact, Your medical bills are facts. Your loss of hair is a fact. Your appearance is a fact.

"On the other hand, God's word is truth. T-R-U-T-H. God's word says, "By His stripes, we are healed." Psalm 103 says, "He heals all of our diseases." The prophet Malachi says there is "healing in His wings." The Scripture says in both Matthew and Luke that, when people sought out Jesus for healing, that "He healed them all." This is truth.

"So the choice you have is this simple: each moment that you endure, you plant your mind and your feet in either the facts or truth. You choose. You choose again. You choose a hundred times a day. You stand in the facts, or you stand in the truth. You can't do both."

How can you not love that?

What the Holy Spirit whispers to you will always, always be the truth. And it is, quite literally, the truth that sets you free.

TRUTH:

In the life of the believer, the Holy Spirit speaks only life and truth.

PRAYER:

Father, I love You! Thank You, God, that You are not the accuser. Thank You that You have not only forgiven my sin but have set me free from every form and voice of darkness. Now, I don't want to be satisfied with less than all that You have for me. I want Your love to pour through me, Your wisdom to pour through me, Your healing power to pour through me, Your acceptance, Your grace, Your generosity, Your deepest knowledge of the innermost currents of men's minds and souls to pour through me. Let me know Your mind and heart in such depth that Your voice echoes in every word I speak. Let me hear and speak truth because You hear and speak only truth. Possess me. Be my God. Be my Guide. Be my Father. I love You.

EXERCISE:

Ask God to give you a supernatural word of encouragement and blessing for someone in your life. As you walk through your days, be attuned to His Spirit. Listen. And, when He prompts you, don't hesitate. Obey. Back up in that little tabernacle against the very sinew and bone of your spinal column, and gently push Him forward. Give Him your mind, your voice, your feet and your hands. Then watch what happens.

Chapter 29

Responding to the Spirit

"For as many as are led by the Spirit of God, they are the sons of God."
Romans 8:14

Have you ever thought about the process that Diana Spencer endured as she was reconstructed into "Princess Diana"?

Having put on the royal mantle which was her new identity, I'm sure Diana suddenly had to see herself in a very different light. She had to walk differently. Her voice had to communicate, in proper English, both authority and grace. She couldn't scratch what itched, hike up what might be slipping, or let loose what bloated her stomach or inflated her bowels. She had to let friends bow and curtsy to her, and serve even those who despised and offended her. She had to learn customs of dozens of cultures and people groups–how to greet them, express thanks, eat properly, where to stand in relation to principals of any group, what titles to use for Pope, Rajah or Sultan, etc. She had to learn grace.

She had to learn to recognize and master facial expressions and body language which may have been fully unconscious up to that point. For example, Diana "adopted the cause" of ridding the world of abandoned land mines. So, in touring hospitals in Cambodia or Eastern Europe and suddenly confronted with a child, wide-eyed and once physically beautiful but now mutilated and broken, she could not wince or lean away in revulsion or horror. How does one not lurch back when confronted with a noxious odor? How does one smile and swallow foreign food over which taste-buds are screaming hysterically, "SPIT IT OUT!"

With perhaps the whole world watching her every move, EVERYTHING Diana did or didn't do defined what it meant to be British to the world. And the entire world, beginning with her mother-in-law the queen, expected her to pull it off with grace and dignity.

How did she do that? What training did she have? Who taught her?

We, as adopted children of God, each go through a similar process under the gentle and quiet tutelage of the Holy Spirit. Just as Diana "put on" the mantle of royalty, so we do the same. "For as many as you as have been baptized into Christ have put on Christ," says Galatians 3:27. And Paul, in Col. 2:6, encourages believers, "As ye have therefore received Christ Jesus the Lord, so walk ye in him."

The good news for us is that we have the best tutor in the world, AND whatever resource we feel we might be lacking at any time He has already bought and delivered for our use.

As my best friend Jeremy was first brought into the one-ness of walking with God, there were some outwardly comical moments. The Holy Spirit would tell him, "Stand up." Then "Sit down." Then "Stand up." Then "Sit down." Four or five times in a row, Jeremy would walk through these exercises as a means, the Holy Spirit explained, for Jeremy to become accustomed to the sound of His voice.

At first, God may tell you to simply move from one chair to another, stand still in a quiet place and calm your heart, take a walk in the middle of the day, get up and close the door, take off your shoes, get on your knees, go sit on the porch, turn off the radio, or a thousand other seemingly irrelevant options.

Once your ears are opened to the sound of His voice, the whole world changes. And perhaps more than any other vital path in your life, this path will lead you out of the foyer of religion into the fullness of the mansion and estate He has given you by inheritance.

As you respond and obey the simplest of commands, the purposes behind His instructions become more clear. The actual content of those instructions takes on real significance. Over time, the simple instructions morph into conversations, discussions of the things that occupy His mind, wisdom regarding the challenges and opportunities of your days, or even predicaments or dangers facing other people.

Here are a handful of important truths of which you should be aware.

First, the purpose of Holy Spirit communication is not simply for your joy and fulfillment but is also to shower grace on others through you. As you learn to respond in confidence to His instructions, supernatural events take place. You will "see" the most profound needs and the deepest motivations of complete strangers. Others will be healed by the touch of your hand or the sound of your voice. People whom you never thought noticed or watched you will turn to you for counsel. Colleagues or family members will find acceptance and peace simply standing in close proximity. Other people, instantly and from very deep within, will hate you for no cause whatsoever. People under the influence or authority of the Kingdom of Darkness will run from you, ignore you, confront you with vulgar gestures or threats, or in other ways despise you.

Second, as you respond to the Holy Spirit, you will grow in your own spiritual gifting. The identification of your particular gifts will become clear, and you will recognize your place within His larger body. The Holy Spirit will even lead you into specific circumstances which will stretch your faith and expand the range of a gift such as healing or prophecy or giving. He Himself will disciple and mature you.

Third, as you see divine gifts bubble up and overflow from others, you can ask the Holy Spirit to give you the gifts you covet. A more recent acquisition in my life is the ability, by touching someone, to actually "see" traumatic circumstances in their earlier life and the lies which the enemy has often planted in the chaos of those traumatic moments. I asked for "prophecy," and this is what He gave me.

Finally, as He leads you into a seamless synchronicity in this amazing Heavenly waltz, you'll find that there are times where He actually lets you lead. Instead of His consistently counseling you as you address the various choices of your life, He will carry you to a position of maturity where the Holy Spirit presents you with choices and tells you, "You choose, and I'll back you either way!"

Religious people will tell you that this is all too dangerous, that you are unfit even to interpret the Scripture accurately, much less to hear and understand the voice of God Himself. It's the line of argument that has, for centuries, empowered legions of illegitimate religious leaders, "false prophets" and "ravenous wolves." (Matt. 7:15) To heed their self-serving teaching would be like Cinderella, settled into the arms and the castle of her prince, hiring as royal life-coaches her evil and disenfranchised step-sisters. Why would anyone empower such people?

Read the words written by the Apostle John to first-century believers: "These things I have written to you concerning those who are trying to deceive you. As for you, the anointing which you received from Him abides in you, and you have no need for anyone to teach you; but as His anointing teaches you about all things, and is true and is not a lie, and just as it has taught you, you abide in Him." (1 John 2:27)

Here's the same Scripture paraphrased in The Message: "I've written to warn you about those who are trying to deceive you. But they're no match for what is embedded deeply within you—Christ's anointing, no less! You don't need any of their so-called teaching. Christ's anointing teaches you the truth on everything you need to know about yourself and him, uncontaminated by a single lie. Live deeply in what you were taught."

As you abide, you will grow and mature. And as you grow and mature, falling ever deeper into love with this astounding indwelling Presence of God, He will draw you into deeper and deeper levels of awareness and power and confidence.

To really walk with in conscious one-ness with God is not a religious exercise. It's a way of life. It's a life destination, not a place you go to rest like a weekend at the beach. One-ness is an adventure really known by very few people.

I'm not sure the Holy Spirit knows any other way to transform us except "from glory to glory." Every day on this journey is an amazing adventure.

Thanks for walking this far with me.

TRUTH:

The guidance of the Holy Spirit is not a single occurrence or some mystical finish line where crowds applause and trophies are distributed. His guidance is an ongoing journey with potential to go on forever.

PRAYER:

My Dear Father, I recognize that coming to know You is not a single prayer, not an instantaneous revelation of truth. I recognize that, like any other relationship, learning to know and hear and respond to Your voice and Presence involves a life-long process. Thank You for Your patience with me. Thank You for the certain knowledge that, from Your perspective far above the limits of time, You see me as the finished product. Thank You that, in my Spirit, I became one with You the moment that I first embraced Your forgiveness. Thank You that You conform my mind more and more to Yours, and that I am not dependent upon my own motives or own energy even in that process. Thank You that You love me. Thank You that, as I mature, I look more and more like my Father. Thank you. Thank you. Thank you.

EXERCISE:

It always amuses me how, the moment a baby is born, women especially possess a gift for seeing the resemblance between the child and his mother, father, grandparents, etc. So let's transfer that into the spiritual realm. Think of the people whom God has used to reveal Himself to you. Think of those people in your life who, in this process of being conformed to the image of the Holy Spirit, have come to "look like" their Heavenly Father. Write one of them a letter and let them know exactly what you see, the various elements of that resemblance. It will bless that person richly.

Walking in Authority & Power

Chapter 30

Spiritual Authority

"The whole creation waits, breathless with anticipation, for the revelation of God's sons and daughters." **Romans 8:19 CEB**

It was three days after Katrina, and our home town, long known for its towering pines and massive oaks, looked like an endless sea of gargantuan Pick-Up Stix. Perhaps 30% of the larger trees had been ferociously ripped up and tossed, sometimes completely airborne, wherever tornado-force winds cast them. In the storm's wake, roads were totally impenetrable until Uncle Sam began buying chain saws for anyone who could get to a Home Depot or Lowes and say, "I want one." Three days after the storm, the wreckage was finally cleared to the point where Debbie and I could pick up our aging parents and evacuate to Tennessee.

Debbie drove ALL day with our sons, ten and eight, in the back seat. Her father, in his 80's and struggling with lung cancer, rode shotgun. As they crossed into Tennessee, her dad told her to pull into a very luxurious resort, that he would cover the cost. So there they were–unwashed for four days, bedraggled, exhausted, legitimate refugees–checking into an elegant four-star resort. As the boys, just glad to be out of the car, began horse-playing in the lobby, Debbie turned her attention away from the registration desk and, in her exhaustion, told them, "Boys! Act rich!" That three word command became the go-to byword in our family for years to come.

Here's the truth: there is a different air around those who know their identity and resources. They act differently. The person who is confident of his abilities and resources wears authority easily. The person who walks in undaunted boldness will find that opportunities seem to magically appear, strangers are more receptive, people are very often eager to cooperate. People don't question the confident.

Today, I want you to grasp four concepts:

First, even in His earliest ministry, Jesus carried this confidence. In Luke 4 as Jesus first steps into ministry, people in Capernaum "were amazed by his teaching because he delivered his message with authority." (vs. 32) When Jesus expels a demon, Luke says, "They were all shaken and said to each other, 'What kind of word is this, that he can command unclean spirits with authority and power, and they leave?'" (vs. 36)

If some naysayer suggests that Capernaum's small-town audience was perhaps easily impressed, then consider John 2:13-25. An itinerant preacher from a cross-roads town in Galilee, Jesus walks into the Court of the Gentiles, the most coveted commercial real estate in all of Jewry. He braids rope into a makeshift lash and, wrecking the stalls of established merchants, He drives the entire populace of this vast exchange pell-mell into the streets. Yet no one physically challenged Him.

Finally, on the night He was betrayed, a mob of religious leaders and as many as 500 (!!!) uniformed Roman soldiers stormed into the Garden of Gethsemane brandishing lanterns, torches and weapons, hunting for Jesus. Jesus, unarmed, walked to meet them. He asked, "Whom do you seek?" They responded, "Jesus of Nazareth." He said simply, "I am," identifying Himself with the name which God Himself invoked when Moses met Him 1200 years before. IMMEDIATELY, the Scripture says, the entire company, hundreds of soldiers and the Jewish political leadership, ALL lurched back and fell to the ground! (John 18:5-6)

No doubt about it. Jesus walked in tremendous confidence.

Second concept. **The confidence and authority that Jesus carried throughout His years of ministry is miniscule, tiny, not to be compared to the confidence and authority which He possesses now.**

All three of the examples listed above–the testimony in Capernaum, the cleansing of the Temple, and the fallen accusers at Gethsemane–all three happen <u>before</u> the cross. These three things happen during Jesus' life in human flesh when the Scripture describes Him as being a man without physical beauty, a man so impoverished that He had no place to lay His head, a man of sorrows, like a lamb led to slaughter, despised and rejected, acquainted with grief, not esteemed by men.

A far different image of the Savior takes shape on OUR SIDE of the cross. Paul writes, when His Father raised Jesus up, "God highly exalted Him, and bestowed on Him the name which is above every name, so that at the name of Jesus every knee will bow." (Phil. 2:9-10) John seems to run out of words describing the risen Christ in Revelation: seated on a throne, appearing in all the crystalline brightness of jasper and fiery sardius, surrounded by an emerald rainbow. The throne itself sits above a crystal sea, and out of the throne emanates lightning and peals of thunder. Twenty-four secondary thrones and fantastic winged creatures surround the throne, singing the praises of the "lamb who was slain," declaring Him WORTHY to receive ALL power and ALL riches and ALL wisdom and ALL might and ALL honor and ALL majesty and ALL blessing–even as their song is echoed by every living creature of Heaven and Earth, under the seas and even from the deepest pits of Hell! (Rev. 4-5)

Third concept. **Jesus NOW holds ALL authority.** Look at the last teaching of Jesus moments before He rose up into Heaven: "ALL authority has been given to me both in Heaven and on Earth, and, lo, I am with you always even to the end of the age." (Matt. 28:18) Wrap your mind around that! ALL authority. The sum total. No left-overs. No residue. No lack. No excuses. No exceptions. ALL authority.

Finally, Concept #4: **The authority of Christ is transferable.** Look as Jesus transfers a measure of His authority to the apostles: "And

Jesus summoned to Him His twelve disciples and gave them power and authority over unclean spirits, to drive them out, and to cure all kinds of disease and all kinds of weakness and infirmity." (Matt. 10:1) Then in Luke 10 as He extends that authority to 70 more: "Now after this **the Lord appointed seventy others**, and sent them in pairs ahead of Him to every city and place where He Himself was going to come. And He was saying to them...'Whatever city you enter and they receive you, eat what is set before you; and **heal those in it who are sick**, and say to them, 'The kingdom of God has come near to you.'" (Luke 10:1-2, 8-9)

Then, zoom forward to the present age. Having transferred authority to the twelve and then the 70, He now transfers authority to US.

You and me.

"And He said to them, "Go into all the world and preach the gospel to all creation...**These signs will accompany those who have believed**: in My name they will cast out demons, they will speak with new tongues; they will pick up serpents, and if they drink any deadly poison, it will not hurt them; they will lay hands on the sick, and they will recover." (Mark 16:15-18)

As believers in the Lord Jesus Christ, you and I are re-created beings. The Lord Jesus Christ–not the Son of Man depicted during His earthly ministry but the risen Lord, the exalted Christ, the Absolute End-all Ruler of the Totality of Heaven and Earth–has taken up residence inside of this temporary housing we call our bodies. He possesses us.

He didn't surrender any portion of His authority to do that. Even as He lives inside of us, He still rules and reigns. Absolutely. With no equal or competition. "ALL AUTHORITY," He said, "has been given to me both in Heaven and on Earth." (Matt. 28:18)

He can and will, longs and yearns to exercise that authority through us–to cast out demons, to heal the sick, to command circumstances in our own lives and the lives of others whenever the Spirit directs, to forgive sins, to calm storms, even to raise up the dead. In fact, the Scripture says,

ALL CREATION waits in breathless anticipation for the unveiling, the revealing, the manifestation of Christ in us as the very sons of God.

In Him, WE are called to rule and reign.

He can and will rule through you...if you let Him.

TRUTH:

It's okay for you to act rich. You're entitled.

PRAYER:

Father, I never thought of myself before as a spiritual power. I never thought of myself before as being empowered by You to cast out demons, heal the sick, even raise the dead. Whoa! And yet, if You indeed live within me as the Scripture indicates, wouldn't that authority simply be part of Your indwelling person and nature? How could I have believed that, when You came into my body, You somehow surrendered your royal Lordship and gifting? Why would I believe that, before You entered into me, You slipped off Your glory like a pair of shoes and entered into me barefoot and lacking? Show me, Father. Increase my faith. Impart supernatural understanding. Let me know you as my Risen Lord and Savior. Let me see your glorious goodness.

EXERCISE:

Order a copy of Kenneth Copeland's excellent book on John G. Lake called *John G. Lake: His Life, His Sermons, His Boldness of Faith.* Alternatives might be *Smith Wigglesworth Devotional*; Norman Grubb's *Rees Howell: Intercessor;* Neil Anderson's *Victory of the Darkness*; or Jeremy Mangerchine's *The Longest Bridge across Water.* Make those books a part of your regular quiet time.

Chapter 31

Exercising Authority

"Standing over her, He rebuked the fever, and it left her." Luke 4:39

Authority is all about real estate.

It's all about political geography, about who governs where.

Wherever the Name of Christ rules, wherever the opposition is held accountable to His authority, the Kingdom of God is there.

Our son, Sam was just 19, entering into his freshman year of college and about as far away from home as he could be, sharing Christ with a handful of people in the suffocating heat and extreme poverty of a remote Indian village. An old Hindu woman in a worn sari had hobbled up to the edge of his audience and suddenly interrupted Sam's interpreter. His interpreter, a young wide-eyed minister named Amit, turned to Sam and said, "She wants your God to heal her knees."

"What's wrong with her knees?" Sam asked.

"I think it's arthritis," said the interpreter. "She says they hurt all the time."

Without hesitation, Sam pushed a stool forward. "Have her sit down here," he said. With the woman seated, Sam asked for and received permission to touch her knees. Crouching down, he placed his hands gently on her legs and began to proclaim His authority in a clear, firm voice: "This is Sam Diamond. I am an adopted son of the God Most High, a brother to the Lord Jesus Christ. The Holy Spirit, God Himself lives inside my body. I carry in my voice, my words, my hand His divine authority. I am entitled, by His Word, to speak on His behalf. I am trained, authorized, equipped and commissioned. I speak now directly to this woman's knees, and, in the name of the Lord Jesus Christ, I command you to be healed NOW. No more pain. No arthritis. No bone spurs. No inflammation. No swelling. No pain. In His Name, I command you, be completely healed NOW!"

He took his hands off of the woman and instructed the interpreter to have her get up and walk. She was healed.

Before long, a friend of the first woman came with the same problem. God healed her too. With the second healing accomplished, people started dragging sick people out of huts all over the village, backing Sam and Melissa, his sole American companion, up into a cattle shed where the flow of people could be controlled. Sam, turning to Melissa, told her, "Melissa, there are too many for me to do this by myself. You've watched twice. Do what I do, and let me know if you have problems." Over the next four hours, everyone Sam and Melissa placed their hands on was healed. Arthritis, back pain, joint pain, vision problems, fevers, partial paralysis and loss of feeling, and a host of other issues simply evaporated under their command. Melissa is now married and living in a crossroads community in Alabama. Sam is a very active senior at LSU.

How did they do that?

Sam understands his own identity and position in Christ, and he acts decisively out of that understanding with confident authority and no hesitation. He understands that the whole vast estate of the Kingdom of Heaven is his inheritance, and he's decided to move out of the foyer and actively possess what God has in fact willed to him. He and Melissa exerted the authority of Christ into a specific geographic area–the hearts and bodies of people in this far-flung Indian settlement–and planted a Kingdom flag there, laying claim to this space for the Kingdom of Light.

For Sam, who has been schooled in this kind of truth for one-fourth of his life, this kind of healing is almost commonplace. Even as he runs between classes at LSU and manages a growing business, he carries the same quiet confidence which characterized the post-resurrection apostles. I find out, often after the fact, about remarkable healings–a business colleague healed over the phone of fibromyalgia, an impoverished woman of hepatitis-C at one of our ministry nights–healings which reflect Sam's awareness of Christ's indwelling presence.

Look again at Romans 5:17. *"For if by one man's offense death reigned by one; much more they which receive abundance of grace and of the gift of righteousness shall reign in life by one, Jesus Christ."*

Look at the first phrase: *"For if by one man's offense death reigned..."* The "one man" is Adam. His offense was his giving into the temptation of the same enemy which you and I face every day. Adam switched his allegiance, transferred his confidence, and consciously reached out for that which God had specifically forbidden. Through Adam's sin, he traded away His dominion (lordship) over the Earth, given to him in Gen. 1:28, handing that to Satan (Luke 4:6), and voluntarily assumed a position in bondage to sin and death. For the first time, Adam knew, in the deepest sense of the word, both good and evil. And Adam biologically passed that legacy, that position of bondage down to ALL of his descendants, right down to you and me. Now look around and try to pick out something which is not subject to death in some form –illness or injury, decay, moth, rust, bleaching of color and withering of form. Take a moment to try to grasp the extent of death's reign.

Now look at the two words, *"much more."* Much more than what? Much more than the evident reign, the expanse and saturation of the power of death! Much more!

"Much more" what?

Now here WE are: *"they which receive of the abundance of grace and of the gift of righteousness."* That's us. That's you and me. That's every born-again believer.

So what's it saying? We–"they which receive of the abundance of grace and of the gift of righteousness"–"**SHALL REIGN IN LIFE!!!**"

How are we to reign? MUCH MORE!

We–you and I–are called to *"REIGN IN LIFE...MUCH MORE"*!

"Much more" than what? Than death!!!! Than Satan!!!! Than every dark form, every malignant manifestation, every poisonous conniving of an enemy who has held men in horrifying bondage since the moment that fatal fruit slid past the first man's "Adam's apple"!

That enemy no longer reigns! Do you get that? WE DO!!! WE REIGN! WE REIGN through the gifting and power and inheritance of the God Who died for us and has chosen, redeemed and anointed us as His royal heirs.

How does death manifest? In what forms does death reveal itself? In illness, injury, cancer, heart disease, diabetes, paralysis and atrophy, mental afflictions, twisted limbs, blind eyes, broken bones, pain, fear and terror, rage and anger, violence, loneliness, shame, isolation, poverty, sexual deviance, illicit cravings, wounded hearts, addictions, feelings of inadequacy–every cause or motivation, every dark consequence of the presence of the enemy on this planet is to be brought under the authority of the Lord Jesus Christ through us as His church on this Earth!

Christ in you reigns over ALL of these things,...if you let Him.

This is your calling. This is your privilege. This is your birthright. This is the power of your inheritance. You have the ability in your new identity in and of Christ to transform the world around you, to triumph over the schemes of the enemy, and to extend the authority of the Kingdom of God to the very limits of your own sphere of influence.

In that light, in that revelation, you can understand Paul's teaching in Romans 8:19-21– *"For the anxious longing of the creation waits eagerly for the revealing of the sons of God. For the creation was subjected to futility, not willingly, but because of Him who subjected it, in hope that the creation itself also will be set free from its slavery to corruption into the freedom of the glory of the children of God."*

This is your inheritance.

Will you now, as Sam does, simply stand up and walk today in it?

TRUTH:

As a believer, you have inherited the authority of God Himself over sin, death and every form of darkness. You simply need to believe and command to see that authority manifest.

PRAYER:

Father, I realize that walking in the divine authority which is my birthright is going to require a new sensitivity to Your voice, perhaps a new measure of courage. Thank you, Father, that You have promised to lead me into all truth and to be my strength when I feel weak. Let me not show that weakness to those to whom I minister nor to the enemy who would seek to limit and oppose me. Make me a minister of Your power and peace.

EXERCISE:

The couple who first taught me about healing run a powerful ministry out of Houston, Texas, called The Elijah Challenge. William & Lucille's calling is to teach ordinary, "faceless" believers how to exercise the authority each one of us possesses because of the Presence of Christ in us. Inspiring missionaries who learned the Biblical exercise of healing while pastoring deep in the jungles of Borneo, William and Lucille now travel and teach around the globe. They wrote their own story in a dramatic 100-page booklet which can be downloaded directly from their website. It's a great, great read. You can download *Dancing on the Edge of the Earth* for free at by simply Googling that title or plugging in the long web address: http://api.ning.com/files/cRZ6JPe-0lpxl1YGcBNz6Fr-sWmeBEjrcQ-5EE*LR3wkcMQii46sE6Y2XvIoVFWF4i78cTYaXD-VXcJxggtePHO4B9Tpw-NVQO/1Dancingontheedgeoftheearth.pdf

Chapter 32

Prophecy: Speaking for the Holy Spirit

"Pursue love, yet desire earnestly spiritual gifts, but especially that you may prophesy." 1 Cor. 14:1

My closest friend is a prophet. It's a thrill to work alongside Jeremy. God constantly whispers to him, carries him places, unfolds visions before him, or even simply causes the supernatural to give way to their interaction so that Jeremy will suddenly see through walls or follow God's direction to a specific store or even a certain streetcar to find someone. He and God share an exciting, continuously refreshing relationship.

So I went through a period of time when I was jealous of his gift. I prayed over and over, "God let me share Jeremy's gift! Let me have that kind of prophetic power and experience!"

One morning in the church where I sneak away to pray, suddenly God spoke with me regarding that request. "Dave," he told me, "Jeremy's gift belongs to Jeremy, and I don't plan on sharing with you in the exact same way. At the same time, I love that you ask, and I want to delineate three very specific gifts that I have for you."

"Whoa!" I breathed, and waited expectantly.

"I have already put power in your hands," He told me. "I have given you long life. And finally, because you ask for prophecy, I have given you the ability to see men's souls."

It took me two weeks to discover what that third gift might mean. One morning, I was leaving a meeting of church leaders in a wonderful church where I had been asked to give some direction. One of the attendees was a woman with an ever-present dog. She was an attorney, polished but comfortable and clearly very intelligent. We really didn't know each other, but she stopped me on the sidewalk outside of the church and asked if I would pray for her. An initial health examination had revealed signs of diabetes, and she was very concerned.

"Sure," I responded. In the nano-second in which my hand first came into contact with her forehead, a flood of impressions and information burst into my mind like confetti from an explosive party favor. I was stunned. My mind raced to grasp what was happening and to make sense of the many floating images. When I could speak, words simply flowed. "Dale," I said, "I'm more than happy to pray regarding your diabetes, but you and I both know that's not the primary issue here."

"What --," she started to speak and then stopped.

"There's a burden, a pressing spiritual weight that you've carried around every day for 25 years," I said, "and God wants to set you free from that. I'm not sure what it is, but it's painful and scary to you and something you think about continuously. He wants to set you free."

Dale stared at me. Then tears welled up. As the first one broke and slid down her cheek, she simply turned and walked away.

Two months later at a Faith & Freedom Ministry Night, God revealed the issue. Twenty-five years before, fresh out of the law school, Dale had been lured into a home appointment where two men were waiting to attack her. Suddenly conscious of their intent, Dale had run away, accelerating her car so quickly that she had hit one of the young men, throwing him up over the hood so that he had slammed into and bounced off of her windshield. Even in her terror, she recounted how she had "watched his lights go out." Dale had not stopped but left the scene entirely, not knowing whether the man was alive or dead.

For 25 years, the "accuser of the brethren" had plagued Dale. Despite diligent searches, she had never found any evidence of the man's death. Nonetheless, the enemy had gained an entrance. For years and then decades, he plagued Dale with continuous accusations that she had murdered that man. It was Dale's secret, dark and dangerous, teeming with fear, and the enemy flogged her mercilessly.

That night, God set Dale free. Over the next week, two people stopped me to ask me, "Dave, what happened to Dale?" One said, "Dale walked into our office the other day, and no one recognized her. Her countenance was so different. It was like someone had given her a face-lift from the inside out, a lightness about her step and voice that none of us had seen or heard before. We asked her what had happened, and she only laughed and said to ask you." Of course, I didn't say, but the evidence of God's work dawning in Dale's life was deeply rewarding.

So what is prophecy? Prophecy is simply speaking out, at God's direction, the words or knowledge which the Holy Spirit imparts.

Understand that there are three levels of prophecy here. (1) All believers can prophecy. (2) Some believers have the spiritual gift of prophecy. (3) And some very few believers are called to be prophets.

Even without the spiritual gift of prophecy which involves a much richer and continuous revelation, every believer can prophesy. If the Holy Spirit lives in you, it's a blind and ignorant assumption to believe that He won't speak to you on a regular basis. As you open your mouth and share the wisdom He provides, you are involved in prophecy. Sometimes, that can take the form of wise counsel. Other times such as the one with Dale, there may be words of knowledge or simply a supernatural form of understanding and empathy Sometimes He may provide just a single word so that you can ask a person, "What I feel like the Holy Spirit is saying is this. What does that mean to you?" Other times, you may receive a single word at first, but then, as soon as you open your mouth, words pours forth. Sometimes, you may suddenly see visions, like daydreams or memories received instantly and in their entirety, and which are clearly relevant to a person or situation at hand.

Two notes about prophecy.

First, on the other side of the cross, Old Testament prophets were usually given messages of condemnation and impending judgment. As we function on this side of the cross, there is no condemnation and none of us, as believers, face the wrath of God's judgment. The purpose of

167

New Testament prophecy is never to accuse, condemn or "convict." The Lord may counsel or caution or warn regarding the wisdom of some action, but He will not accuse or condemn. He can not accuse us of that which He has already forgiven and sworn to "remember no more." (Heb. 8:12, 10:17) It is the enemy, the Devil, who is "the accuser of the brethren, accusing them before our God day and night." (Rev. 12:10) Prophecy is not imparted for you to be a mouthpiece for the devil.

So what is the purpose of prophecy? That's point number two. According to the Apostle Paul, the purpose of prophecy is "edification and exhortation and consolation." (1 Cor. 14:3)

"Edification" is defined in the "Blue Letter Bible" as "the act of building up" or "the act of one who promotes another's growth in wisdom, piety, happiness and holiness."

"Exhortation" is literally a "calling near" as if you were calling someone into a position of confidence or favor. Synonyms include "supplication," "entreaty," "admonition or encouragement," "consolation" or "that which affords comfort or refreshment." The Greek word for exhortation is closely related to one of the names Jesus uses for the Holy Spirit, that is "the Comforter" or "Paraclete." (John 14:16, 26; 15:26 and 16:7)

Finally, the Greek word translated as "consolation" comes from a Greek word meaning to comfort. The Greek word is used only four times in the New Testament, two of those in John 11 when friends of Mary and Martha came to "comfort" the sisters over the death of their brother, Lazarus.

"Edification." "Exhortation." "Consolation." Doesn't sound much like judgment, does it? Condemnation? Accusation? I don't think so.

Prophecy is the first among gifts because, if you can't hear God, you can't obey God. And, once you become accustomed to His voice, speaking into the lives of others is both easy and powerful.

Rest in Him. Pray. Listen. Then simply let it happen.

TRUTH:

Every believer should prophecy. Every believer is empowered to hear the voice of God and speak forth the words and visions God imparts in order to comfort and edify and encourage others.

PRAYER:

Father, in your Word, You said, "My sheep hear My voice, and I know them, and they follow Me." (John 10:27) I am your sheep, Father. I am your child. My desire is to follow You. I know You speak to me through the Scripture, but I long to hear Your voice. I yearn to become so familiar with the sound and intonation of Your voice that listening becomes second nature to me. I long to be aware of Your slightest whisper, Your gentlest touch. I want to hear You laugh, hear You say my name, hear You speak that Your love for others might be made complete through me. Speak to me, Father. Tune my ears to the perfect pitch of Your voice and help me, always, to follow You.

EXERCISE:

Many believers find that keeping a journal of their quiet time with God is very helpful in discerning His voice and recognizing the reality of that supernatural relationship over an extended period of time. Sometimes God speaks even as we write so that, for moments at a time, words of blessing pour out through our hands and sometimes shock us with their clarity and pointed instruction. Understand always, however, this caution: the same technique of "spirit writing" is used by those who worship or give place to evil spirits. Remember that the purpose of prophecy is to build up, edify, instruct and console. The Holy Spirit never accuses, never condemns, never speaks in contradiction to the whole of Scripture. As you listen or write, use these guidelines to discern between the voice of the Holy Spirit and potential voices of darkness.

Chapter 33

Deliverance: "They Shall Cast Out Demons"

"These signs will accompany those who have believed: in My name they will cast out demons." **Mark 16:17**

In the Western church, deliverance–exercising divine authority to command demonic spirits–is probably the most overlooked and neglected of all spiritual activities.

According to Barna Research, the most widely respected polling group on issues of faith, 40% of self-identified Christians don't believe Satan exists, and another 19% "agree somewhat' with the statement that Satan "is not a living being but is a symbol of evil."

Hmm-m-m.

In my own experience, Satan manifests in brute force in those cultures such as Hindu India of Sub-Saharan Africa where the open acknowledgement of spiritual beings is commonplace. In the Western world, the enemy relies much more on deception and works undercover, so that those who are afflicted–and I've ministered to many–hide what they experience or submit to physicians who use chemical means to curb the frothy crests of demonic rage or terror or suicidal compulsions. In doing so, they often not only fail to vanquish the oppressor but also bury the oppressed person's beauty and joy under layers of chemical lassitude.

We need to know that the enemy is real and intent upon owning the hearts and minds of men. He seethes, not out of any appreciation at all for humankind but out of unimaginable hatred for God and therefore a consuming desire to destroy and steal from God that which God values most highly. That esteemed possession is us.

We need to know his tactics. As discussed earlier, we blame a vast host of ills upon "the devil," but, in the end, he only holds two weapons. Just as the world's most complex computers "think" using a binary language with only two characters (zero and one), so all the enemy's machinations rely upon only two weapons: lies and accusations.

Especially in times of trauma, the enemy attacks and plants, sometimes into our deepest subconscious, lies and accusations. Once received and embraced, his lies and accusations blossom and bear fruit in reprehensible behavior that then provides fallow ground for more of his lies.

A woman, for example, molested by her father or step-father then very often believes that she has no authority over her own body, that this authority belongs to any person strong enough to assert himself with power or confidence. As one victim told me, "Dave, my dad stole my 'No' from me. I grew up under the unconscious assumption that my body didn't belong to me, that it belonged to others–especially domineering men–and therefore I had no right to say 'No.'"

Promiscuity then compounds the pain and provides fertile ground for more lies and accusations. "My only value," the woman continued, "lay in the act of sex. But, even as I performed or consented, each time was a deep scream, a pleading for some sort of appreciation, some level of acceptance. It never worked. In the end, I was always a little bit dirtier, a little more ashamed. a little less human than before I had begun."

The secret to deliverance lies in the truth of John 8:31-32. The law Jesus set forth here is as sure and consistent as the law of gravity: "the truth will set you free." (John 8:32)

Deliverance is simple. With clear confidence in the indwelling Presence of the Holy Spirit, ordinary Christians have the right to proclaim Scriptural truth over those who are spiritually oppressed or possessed. We have the power, under His authority, to command demonic powers to be bound and sent to judgment.

More often, there is a process in which, by carefully and prayerfully listening to the oppressed person, lies from which the enemy has constructed his stronghold come to light. By identifying those lies out loud and, in love, replacing those lies with the truth, we can deconstruct the enemy's stronghold. By speaking truth and proclaiming the love, forgiveness and acceptance of Christ, we can dismantle the enemy's house. With that done, then we can order the enemy himself to vacate the premises, to pack up and ship out, to surrender and go to Christ for judgment.

Usually, that's a fairly quiet process. In rare cases, there is some physical manifestation such as choking and/or coughing; muscle spasms or sudden excruciating pain usually in the back or abdomen; vomiting or discharge of mucus from the nose or mouth; shuddering, shaking or physical contortions; laughter or mockery sometimes in a voice other than the victim's own; screaming of religious exclamations; growling or howling; cursing or profanity; threats of physical harm to myself or my family; or, finally, attempts by the victim to hurt or even kill himself or herself. The victim may be in a state of complete unconsciousness to his or her own actions, "waking up" afterward with no memory of what just transpired. Most, however, are very much aware and awake throughout the process and will, if asked, take part by repeating after me professions of their own faith and rejection of every harassing spirit of darkness.

In a very small number of cases in my experience, the deliverance process can last for hours or, in even fewer cases, days.

In deliverance, prayer support is critical. If I have time to prepare, I try to have at least one more person present and, sometimes, two or three. We try to meet at the person's home, for these reasons: (1) the appearance of the home will tell you a lot about the enemy involved; (2) sometimes the demonic power can be rooted or anchored to the home itself; (3) the person undergoing deliverance is usually more comfortable in his or her home environment; and (4) the home provides an environment of privacy and safety that an office, church or hospital room can't afford. You don't want to do deliverance at WalMart.

Afterward, you want to follow-up with that person. Even after the enemy is evicted, we must recognize that the adversary has enjoyed months or years in which he can foster habits, engender reactions, re-route the synapse patterns of the brain so stimuli like the smell of drugs, for example, or even the time at which a repetitive abuser customarily arrived can trigger denigrating behavior. The echoes of lies and accusations re-open old wounds and afford the enemy fresh opportunities to oppress even if those opportunities are fleeting and short-lived.

The good news is that the taste of divine peace, love and freedom are so ferociously intoxicating that a person, once delivered, will usually fight to remain so. New life dawns. Acceptance and love engender self-respect, faith and hope. The ability to rest in Him ultimately triumphs.

In the end, we can anchor ourselves into Christ through the heart acceptance of just two or three truths.

The first is our one-ness God Himself, facilitated by the Scripture but maturing into a moment-by-moment relationship.

The second is this miracle: He loves us. He loves us. He clothed His own Son in human flesh and then allowed us to rip that flesh to shreds, sowing into His wounds the mucus and venom of our own misplaced rage. He let us nail His only Son's body as an open spectacle to a tree. This was His sacrifice to forgive ALL of our sins. He has forgiven ALL of our sins—past, present and future—and, in that, gained the legal right to unite with us and show Himself through us.

The third is this: because we are one spirit with Him, we share in His authority over every circumstance, every power, every being that has ever been or ever will be on the Earth. We—you and I—can command every other spiritual being to obey us in accordance with that authority. In Him, we hold a thousand times more power than we have ever experienced or even thought possible.

It's up to us to use it as He, the Holy Spirit, directs.

TRUTH:

In Christ, we have authority over every force of darkness. Learning to wield that authority must be a Spirit-led process.

PRAYER:

Father, how good and glorious You are! How rich and generous! How careful and compassionate! Thank You that You are Lord, that I can rest in the shadow of Your wings. Thank You that Your commitment to Abraham to be His shield, His protector, (Gen. 15:1) was a commitment to me as well. Thank You that, in You, I have been lifted up inside Christ and placed at the right hand, the power hand of the Father in Heaven, that I have by Your grace a measure of Kingdom authority. Teach me, Holy Spirit, not only to know this truth but to walk in ever-increasing awareness and effectiveness. Use me, Lord, as a force for the Kingdom of God, to be a part of Your grace in "calling many sons to glory."

EXERCISE:

You don't want to venture into this area without more knowledge and the tutelage of the Holy Spirit. There are books out there which may be very helpful but should be read with prayer and discernment. Some of the best of those are books by Neil Anderson or Leanne Payne. Derek Prince wrote an interesting book called *They Shall Expel Demons*, and Frank and Ida Hammond co-authored an enduring work called *Pigs in the Parlor.* Once again, William & Lucille's *Dancing on the Edge of the Earth* can be downloaded for free and is a great, great testimony.

I provide two-day seminars on healing and deliverance which God has used to transform and empower many churches, almost entirely to this point in India. Contact me for more information in this regard.

Pray and ask the Holy Spirit to lead you into this area. Listen to Him very, very carefully.

Chapter 34

Healing: "They Shall Lay Hands on the Sick."

"These signs will accompany those who have believed: in My name...they will lay hands on the sick, and they will recover." **Mark 16:17-18**

Most Christians don't understand this truth:

There is no record that Jesus ever prayed for the sick. There is no reference where Peter, Paul, John, any of the other apostles, Stephen, Phillip, or any of the other principal characters of the New Testament ever healed the sick by praying for them. (See note at chapter's end)

What Jesus did was heal people. What Peter did was heal people. What John did was heal people. What Stephen did was heal people. Apparently healing was accomplished NOT by praying but by commanding, drawing upon spiritual authority that lay within their one-ness with the Lord of the Universe. Because Christ lived in them, they possessed in Him the authority to speak and then expect the spiritual and physical world around them to conform to the power of their words. There was, is, and always will be a huge place and need for prayer. I believe in prayer. But the principal characters of the New Testament, confronted with the immediate presence of a sick or injured person, did not apparently pray in order to restore that person to health.

Why?

Understand and receive this. Every action Jesus took through three years of ministry can be broken down into one of three offices. Jesus was (1) priest, (2) prophet and (3) king.

So what does a priest do? The position of a priest is to facilitate relationship between God and men. For that reason, I like to illustrate the priestly role with a simple arrow pointing straight up. Priests hold that halfway position, "pointing" men to God and serving God among men. Within that office then, the functions of a priest include prayer, intercession, praise, worship, sacrifice, etc.

What does a prophet do? The domain of a prophet involves the administration and exercise of spiritual gifts such as preaching, teaching, administration, giving, helps, prophecy, tongues and the interpretation of tongues, etc. As discussed in Chapter 32, the role of a prophet is to listen to the voice of God and speak or act in accordance with God's instruction for the purpose of building up of the church and the edifying of saints. For that reason, I like to illustrate the functions of the prophetic office with a simple horizontal arrow. Prophets obey God but their ministry lies in serving the people, especially the saints, who surround them.

What do kings do? Kings go to war. They exercise spiritual authority. They advance the dominion of the Lord whom they serve. In His kingly office, Jesus commanded demons, and they obeyed Him. In His kingly office, he rebuked fevers and paralysis and leprosy and palsy, and people were healed. Kings exercise authority, best pictured by an arrow pointing down.

Healing and deliverance are acts of war. They are the extension of God's command over circumstances in which some form of darkness has intruded and found temporary residence. The enemy's means of entry are always deception and accusation. The enemy's intent is always to harass, to steal, to kill and destroy. The purpose of God, acting through us, is to undo the actions of the enemy. "The Son of God appeared for this purpose: to destroy the works of the devil." (1 John 3:8)

For this reason, when a sick person lies before me or sits on the other end of a telephone connection, I don't focus on prayer. It's not a time for prayer. Prayer is a priestly function, and the situation before me is a call to war. Like Sam, I identify myself by declaring the truth of God regarding Christ's authority and His Presence in me. Then, with identity and authority established, I command dark powers to leave, and illness and injury to be healed. I exercise authority. Results—especially now that I have been practicing healing and deliverance for several years–are usually immediate, especially in ministry to non-believers.

When David ran out onto the field of battle to face the Philistine giant, Goliath, David didn't fall on his knees and pray. Faced with the nine-foot armored behemoth, David didn't shut his eyes, speak in tongues, dance in worship or sing hymns of praise. He didn't look for his anointing oil or call for support. He didn't try to teach, preach, minister, administrate, prophecy or convert Goliath. He picked up stones, ran forward, attacked and killed Goliath. He took Goliath's head off.

David understood the favor which he carried with God because of his experience as the family shepherd, killing a bear and a lion. On this foundation of faith and experience, he then RAN forward to wrench the life out of the heathen behemoth and send the nine-foot freak to eternal judgment. Even in his later life as king of Israel, David did not send his priests or his prophets to do battle; he sent his "mighty men."

In the same way, healing is war–not against some gargantuan Philistine, but against a foe vanquished 2000 years ago when God Who loves us offered His back, His ribs, His muscle, His spine to the lacerating leather of the Roman lash. "For by His wounds, you have been healed." (1 Peter 2:24 NASB)

When we go into battle, we use the same weapon Jesus did–His voice. Just as by His spoken word, entire realms of life came into being, so, by His word spoken through us, illness and injury are healed. The Scripture repeatedly refers to the Word of God as being a sword, an offensive weapon. In Revelation when John sees Christ enthroned as the Lord of Lords, John says, "Out of His mouth went a sharp two-edged sword." (Rev. 1:16) Jesus gave us the use of that sword when He transferred a measure of His own authority to us. Because we fight by spiritual means, we wage war by speaking, by rebuking, by commanding compliance with those things which God has already done and declared to be true. By the authority of Christ in us, we command compliance to the fullness of His authority. People then are healed and delivered.

In the practical application of this truth, I don't simply walk up to people and ask them if I can command them to be healed. It would be nice if that worked, but it doesn't. I ask them humbly if I might "pray" for them. Very few people turn down prayer. Once permission is granted, I ask if I can rest one of my hands on the person's back or shoulder or forehead, always conscious of propriety and the fears or feelings of the sick person. I begin with prayer, asking God's blessing and reminding Him of all of the promises which we possess in the Scripture.

Then speaking very clearly, I say something like, "Now, <u>turning away from prayer</u> and turning to specifically address the illness (injury) before me, I assert the authority of Christ who lives in me and command this illness to be gone NOW from this person, never to return." Sometimes I address symptoms or specific areas of pain. And I almost always end by commanding, "Now, in the authority of Jesus, be healed!"

Healing happens. Sometimes right away. Sometimes in minutes or a couple of hours or two or three days or longer. Terminal illnesses are healed. Doctors are sometimes mystified. People are set free.

At first, the "success rate" of such activities probably hovered around 20% to 30%. As I have grown in faith and experience, now I would think 70% or 75% of the people to whom I minister are healed or at least relieved of symptoms. Every experience holds new lessons to learn. There is still so much I don't understand. But I have found that God's Word is true, and His authority rests within me at all times, easily accessible to exercise in any field of battle.

You, as a believer, share that same authority.

He has given you this power.

Please, use it as He directs.

TRUTH:

As children adopted into the family of God, we have been granted the authority to heal the hurts and illnesses of others.

PRAYER:

Father, You are a God who heals. Because You live in me, I receive and believe that this power as well resides within me. How can it be otherwise? Teach me, Father, to exercise this power and to minister effectively that other people might experience the grace and goodness, the forgiveness and one-ness which You have shared so freely with me.

EXERCISE:

Our friends, William and Lucille, work through a ministry called The Elijah Challenge. They have a huge website, stuffed chock full with testimonies of the people whom they have taught in the areas of healing and deliverance.

William and Lucille still teach healing in countries all around the world. Now I do as well. So does John G. Lake Ministries–they have an online course–and, I'm sure, many others.

If you'd like to participate in a two-day class with me or arrange for me to come and teach within your church or home group, contact me via the internet at dave@davediamond.net.

Note: James, in his epistle, instructs believers to seek out the church elders for prayer OVER the sick, indicating perhaps the practice of Paul the Apostle in Acts 28:7-8 where Paul is asked to heal the father of Publius. The Scripture says that Paul "entered in, prayed, AND laid his hands on him, AND healed him." The grammatical structure indicates that entering in, praying, laying on of hands, and then healing were all separate but related activities. In like manner, Jesus prayed BEFORE he commanded Lazarus to come forth from the grave. Even in his prayer, He suggests that the prayer was unnecessary but spoken for the benefit of "the people which stand by...that they may believe that You have sent Me." (John 11:41-43)

Chapter 35

Rest!

"There remains therefore a rest for the people of God." **Heb. 4:9**

My prayer is that this book has been a blessing to you. My prayer is that you will recognize value here and encourage others to pick it up and read. It's an awful thing to spill your heart out on to page after page, wondering whether anyone will be blessed through your effort. Your reading completes this process, and I am blessed by your attention.

Our second son, Luke, attends one of the world's most prestigious acting schools. As he studies theater and reads voluminous amounts of literature, Luke has developed an intense love of the power of words. For this reason, as he talks, I'm always very conscious of his vocabulary.

Several times, I noticed that, in pursuing his craft, Luke uses the word "MOMENT" as a verb. In a short essay which he presented to Debbie and me as a Christmas present, he included the sentence, "On my chalkboard in my dormitory, I write quotes that moment in my life."

"To moment," then, is to allow yourself to be drawn body, soul and spirit into a singular instant of time so that you experience that particular circumstance to the very fullest measure. "To moment" is to voluntarily surrender EVERYTHING else to suck the marrow of life out of a fraction of a second, to see and taste and hear and feel the nano-second of a passing experience. An actor on a stage will "moment" in a particular scene so that all of his existence is confined precisely to the here and now. A world-class pitcher will "moment" on the mound in order to execute the perfect fastball and, in doing so, claim Game Seven of the World Series. To "moment" is to embrace that immediate instant to the fullest measure of appreciation, to inhale experience second-by-second as an 140-proof elixir and then appreciate it's cyclonic rush coursing through your veins.

I want to "moment" with God continuously.

The most absurdly miraculous thing is that my thirst, my passion, my longing is deeply appreciated and wholeheartedly returned by Him.

He LOVES me. He LOVES you. He LOVES us.

The Scripture says the greatest commandment is to love God with your entire heart, soul, mind and strength. Once you know Him, however–once you have abandoned all "self-ness" and fallen back into the furious tsunami of his whole-hearted embrace–how can anyone not love God?

The harder issue for me is simply to rest.

At age 62, I've been granted the outrageous privilege of being able to see people as God Himself sees them. Each one, regardless of their warped perspectives or twisted and tortured history, was created in infinite beauty, knit together in ribbons of empassioned love, planned for and anticipated since before God first shouted photons of light into being. Each person holds limitless promise, possesses gifts of astounding magnitude, and encapsulates the power to carry the very heart of his Creator into the moment-by-moment hurly-burly of other people's lives. Like the world's most gifted matchmakers, we get to introduce this Person, this amazing passionate God, to people whom He already loves but who have never known Him before. We get to share Him with others.

There's simply not enough time.

The confines of height, breadth, depth and time are too narrow. And so I run. I rush. I over-commit. I tend to make impossible promises. Sometimes I double-book appointments, and I feel guilty, as full as my life is, in not finding time to share with this one or that one or everyone.

In the rush, I lose sight of essential truths, and my heart begins to bend toward stress and worry. Unfounded questions nag and drive me to more commitments, more interaction, and less time for rest.

I have to remind myself, "Dave, BEFORE you are a husband or a father or a healer; before you are a teacher, a preacher, a marketing agent, an author, artist or minister; before you are a cook and bottle-washer, an amateur mechanic, a source of tuition revenue or a fix-it man–before you are ANY of these things, you are just a son. You are His child!"

My Father loves me.

He is proud of me.

He sees infinite value in me.

He has amazing plans for me, plans far beyond even the furthest threshold of this life, this planet, this universe.

He has paid a huge price for the joy of my companionship.

I can rest now in Him.

A while back, our oldest son, Sam, called me up to ask me a question. "Dad," he said, "feel like driving with me to Dallas tomorrow?"

"Wow, Sam! What's in Dallas?"

"I've got a meeting to go to, Dad. There's really nothing for you at all at this point except maybe the ride."

I smile even now because Sam understands. It's eight hours to Dallas and eight more to come back. But he's my son. If he asked me, "Hey, want to take a drive to Juneau, Alaska?" I'd do my best to break free and ride along.

I get to be with my son.

I get to watch his face as he talks to me about his plans, his friends, his successes and challenges at work. I'll marvel at his physical beauty, always thinking, "My God, he must have inherited that from his mother!" I'll notice again the wrinkle in the top of his left ear, a trait that he's held on to since he first eaked through his mama's blood and water and squalled his first breath. I'll see the scar above his right eyebrow, a reminder of a bar-fight on the occasion of his 21st birthday. I'll listen to his words and see his facial expressions, but I'll also be aware of his accent, his energy, the grab-your-heart blue of his eyes, the joy he takes in his shoulder-length hair, his love of country music, the confidence in his smile, the sound of his chuckling laughter.

The drive, the distance, the weather, even the reason doesn't matter. It's all small potatoes, motes of swirling dust in the greater frame of life.

What I know is this: I would drive to the outer limits of Hell to spend a day with my either one of my sons. I would go into casinos, brothels, torture chambers, insane asylums, third-World slums, crack houses or maximum security prisons to spend a few hours with my son. I would pay for time with my son and, no matter what the asking price, consider it a bargain. I would sit through rap concerts, opera performances, elementary dance recitals, dental appointments, the Ice-capades, wrestling matches, shouting contests, even conventions for Christian television personalities to share time with my son.

I love my sons.

And that's the way God loves me.

I am His child.

You are His child.

For as long as we're on this crazy trip together, we can rest entirely in Him.

He loves us.

TRUTH:

The secret to power in life is learning to rest in one-ness with Him.

PRAYER:

Thank You, Father, for being just that–my Father. Thank You for Your love and confidence. Thank You for grace. Lead me forward, Lord. Lead me into a greater appreciation for all that You have done for me. Let me walk in Your grace and wisdom every day. Let others see You in me even as I learn to rest in You. I love You. Thank You for loving me first. Thank you.

EXERCISE:

I would love to know your reaction to this book. I would love to know your questions and your suggestions regarding this work. You can contact me at dave@davediamond.net. It would also help me tremendously if you also ventured on-line to Amazon and placed a thoughtful review of this work on the record there.

God bless you.

He loves you so much.

About the Author

Dave Diamond is a minister without a seminary degree, a pastor without a church, a teacher without a school, a counselor without an office...and he kind of likes it that way. A graduate of Marquette University and Richmond College near London, England, Dave now travels around the globe, teaching the love of Christ, healing, deliverance, and the "how-to's" of effective evangelism. He, his wife Debbie and their sons, Sam and Luke, call the New Orleans area home. Dave can be reached by e-mail at dave@davediamond.net. To discuss a speaking or teaching engagement, please contact Dave via e-mail or Facebook.